Everyday Courage

Finding Bravery in Life and Motherhood

J ENNIFER H ENDRIX

PAGE PUBLISHING, INC.
Conneaut Lake, PA

First originally published by Page Publishing 2020

ISBN 978-1-64701-880-1 (pbk)
ISBN 978-1-64701-881-8 (digital)

Printed in the United States of America

To my mother, who always believed I could achieve great things.
To my husband, for insisting I would never
have time to write this book.
To Maxwell and Vivian, for giving me the greatest gifts of my life.
To the Mama reading this book, this one's for you.

CONTENTS

Let's start out by saying, I am no expert. On anything really. I don't have a fancy degree in child development or psychology. I don't have fifteen years of experience in the field. I am in no position to guide you through your early years of motherhood and life after motherhood whatsoever. So if you're looking for expert advice from actual experts, this book isn't for you. Maybe you can regift it for Christmas next year? I wrote this book because it's what I would have wanted to read when my children were babies. This book is a collection of my war stories that are in no particular order because my mom brain cannot chronologically organize them. If you enjoy books that flow together from start to finish with perfectly selected quotes to start each chapter, skip this read.

I want to discuss the fundamental truths about motherhood. I'm not talking about the greatest accomplishment of your life or the reason you get out of bed in the morning. I'm talking about the raw side of motherhood. The good, the bad, and the ugly. It is only when we begin to talk about these things openly and without shame (that part is super important) that they will become normalized in our society.

If you were anything like me, pregnancy was filled with reading countless books, magazines, and news articles, and attending as many child preparation courses as I could sign up for, including everything from breastfeeding to child development. I even insisted that my husband attend daddy boot camp and prepared to quiz him on everything I found in the book Husband-Coached Childbirth. I thoroughly read The Bradley Method and exercised all the right muscles. My husband believed I was borderline psychotic. (That's okay. He already knew that when he married me, right?) I was convinced that if I gathered as much information as I possibly could, this child was going to be born a neurosurgeon and be making his own breakfast by age two. According to my mother-in-law, my husband was potty-trained by one, so in my mind, anything was possible. I found it vital to learn everything there was about the process of being pregnant. Hello, I was growing eyeballs and a heart over here. I was essentially a pregnant sponge that soaked up as much information as my pregnant, premom brain could handle.

What I failed to read was anything about life after pregnancy. I distinctively remember the nurses discharging us from the hospital and personally asking them if they would come home with us. I bawled my eyes out when they said they could not. I looked at them and said, "You're going to let us take this thing home with us? How will we ever keep it alive?" After parting ways from the hospital, the ride home had to be the worst anxiety I had ever experienced. One, our new baby wasn't exactly easy. Two, my husband's NASCAR driving didn't help.

What exactly was it like to have a baby? How would my life change in ways that I didn't even know possible? How would I work my day job, be a busy mother, be a loving wife, and be Suzy Homemaker? This balancing act was building up to be quite the challenge. All the while receiving unwanted information from every grandmother, mother-in-law, and human on the face of the earth. I clearly had no idea what I was doing, but the overload of information didn't seem to help. In fact, the more information and guidance I received on how to raise this tiny human, the more overwhelmed and overworked I became.

I used to think I was the one with the problem. I used to ponder why all these other moms seemed to have it all together and I was over here on the struggle bus. I was convinced that every mother other than me was drinking half their body weight in water each day, they never missed their morning sweat sesh, and their marriages were made of the stuff you read about in books. I used to sit in the bathroom and bawl my eyes out, wondering when it was going to get better. My poor husband didn't know how to help me either. I was in this torturous cycle of feeding the baby, sleeping, housework, and repeat. I remember having nightmares that my child was still sleeping on my chest even though he was nowhere in sight. I didn't know what day it was, whether it was morning or night, and I smelled of dried breastmilk. My boobs were so sensitive, even the water from the shower made them ache. My only contest of the day consisted of how large my freezer stash of milk was becoming. The right boob was always the loser, and the left never settled for second place. Every day was Groundhog Day, and that damn animal was never going to see its shadow.

Being home with a newborn baby was one of the loneliest places on earth. I was one of the first in my group of friends to have a child. I didn't get a lot of advice or guidance from them because they hadn't yet blazed that trail. I didn't want to be first. I wanted the mommy manual spelled out with all the dos and don'ts. My friends, on the other hand, were overjoyed that I was first. They had front row seats to the shit show that was about to take place, with the lead actor never having rehearsed for the show. No one really understood what I was going through. I felt so alone. I was an emotional rollercoaster that never came to a complete stop. All the emotional ups and downs that happened during pregnancy didn't help the situation. I was elated to be pregnant, but there were times when I was scared shitless. Looking back, I should have paid someone who was pregnant at the same time I was to be my friend so that we could share stories and support one another through pregnancy. When you are in the thick of the forest, having someone with you makes your journey through it not seem so lonely. No one told you that your entire body was going to plump up like a fresh-filled birthday balloon, you couldn't shave anything past your armpits, and you were always in need of fresh underwear or "freshies" as one of my girlfriends called them. I spent time googling why my lady parts were swollen like I just got my tonsils out, if I would ever have an enjoyable bathroom experience ever again, and why my face had developed something call melasma.

When my son was born, I remember watching The Today Show and Rachael Ray religiously. It became part of my maternity leave routine, and I couldn't miss it. I awed at how put together these people looked and how worry-free everyone appeared. I wondered what it would be like to leave the house, but then I realized that I hadn't washed my hair in three days and that I probably better just stay put. Leaving the house involved supplies, an unbelievable amount of things for this tiny human, plus making myself presentable, which was a long, drawn-out task. I breastfed and I bottle-fed, and the countless hours that I spent on Google was sickening. I Googled all day long about whether this was normal or that was normal. I collected so many different opinions on everything that by the end of my search, I was so confused I didn't even remember what I originally typed into the search bar. But Rachael, she was my dedicated friend who was always there for me, she brightened my day with her amazing smile and killer dishes. And that energy. Where did she get all that positive energy from?

I wish my hours would have been spent seeking advice from other new moms or reading a good book instead of spending hours on Google. It takes a village, right? I propose to you, instead of using a search engine for all the time you're breastfeeding or bottle-feeding, read this book and know that there are thousands of other women just like you who are trying to make it to the next day. I remember feeding my baby at all hours of the night, and there was something about seeing that 5:00 a.m. on the clock that made me feel like I made it. I made it through another night. I survived feedings and diaper changes and a fussy baby. I had to enjoy my small victories. After all, they were all I had. I hope this book can be your close group of girlfriends. My wish is that you find hope, assurance, and peace of mind knowing that you are not alone in this, my friend. In fact, it is quite the opposite.

There are so many things my older, wiser self would have told my postpregnant self. You deserve better. Your child deserves better. I hope this book helps you feel like you have a friend in this and someone who has been through it who wants to give you honest, real, and sincere guidance. You may not agree with everything I have to say, and that's okay. My hope is that you laugh and cry the whole way through.

You are more than a mother. You have goals and aspirations. Don't give up on your own self-worth because you feel the need to replace it with your child's. You can have both. You will have both. My goal is that after reading this book, you find at least one valuable piece that you can use on your journey to finding yourself in this crazy thing we call motherhood.

Instead of starting this book with the first chapter, which is "Birthing Life," I need to take you back to the very beginning. Without visiting the beginning first, you won't understand where I started and where I am now. You will only see the end result, and there is so much that happened before I arrived to where I am today. If I start with the first chapter, you will likely think I somehow had a prestigious upbringing, special treatment, more opportunities, or I was somehow born lucky. None of that is true. I am just like you. I work hard. I take chances. I research what I don't know. I stay in my lane. I keep my head down. I work tirelessly on my goals. I am not special. I have nothing more than what I was given, which is my name and my work ethic. I don't have extraordinary super powers. The difference is I had the courage to begin. I took one step forward and then another. I stayed inspired and dedicated to the goals I wanted to achieve. You have that desire too. You just need to stop waiting for it to happen and begin exactly where you are right now.

I grew up in a town thirty minutes west of Springfield, Illinois. I was born in the late 1980s. I was an only child, and I like to say that "my parents stopped at perfection," but we all knew that wasn't the case. All my aunts and uncles lived within ten miles of my parents' house. I was the first grandchild born on both sides. I kid you not, my family called me Baby Jesus. Maybe that was where things started to go wrong, but that's a story for a different day. My mother stayed home with me until I was seven years old. Our days were filled with playdates, gymnastics, ballet, baton twirling, Girl Scouts, tap dancing, and endless amounts of snuggling. In our down time, the small-town housewives of the neighborhood watched All My Children while the kids ate chips and dip and played with Barbies. My mother volunteered for everything. She was the local Girl Scout troop leader, lunch lady, Sunday school coordinator, homeroom mother, and anything else she could volunteer to do so we could spend more time together. Even if it was just a simple wave in the lunchroom or helping me pick out the library book I wanted to take home for the week, my mother was present. My father worked as a welder for almost all my life. He had a long line of mental health problems in his family, and his depression and anxiety worsened after the loss of his father. My father and mother separated when I was seven years old. I didn't understand it at the time, but I was absolutely thrilled to move in with my grandmother until Daddy started feeling better. Little did I know that we would never live together ever again. We didn't have much money growing up, but I never went without anything. My mother worked two jobs to make ends meet. With nothing more than a high school diploma, her job opportunities were limited. She worked at a dental lab for years, making $5.50 an hour while cleaning houses on the side. I remember going with her to hundreds of homes that had outdoor pools, massive kitchens, and enough square footage to fit four families inside. I would split my time between doing homework and helping her clean. She insisted that I didn't have to help, but I always did. If she was going to work this hard for me, the least I could do was help her when I was able. In my mind, the sooner we were done, the sooner we could leave. From a very early age, I was taught the meaning of hard work. My mother could work circles around anyone. She was the Energizer Bunny who never got tired and never needed time for herself. She was a loyal servant and dedicated worker. She amazed me with how much she could get accomplished in such a short amount of time. She didn't have to teach me anything about hard work. She showed me firsthand in the grueling hours she worked in a non-air-conditioned work space. She showed me how to leave work at five o'clock at night and then start her second job. She never had time to sit down and relax. She was always moving and always on her feet. After her second job was complete, she raced home to get me bathed and ready for bed just to do the exact same thing the next day.

She was an absolutely incredible mother. She always put my needs ahead of her own. She would go without new sunglasses, clothes, or a purse if it meant sending me to summer basketball camp. She would wear tennis shoes with holes in them if it meant sending me to a Catholic grade school. She would wear holes in her underwear for months if it meant buying me the new matching team basketball shoes. She would clean extra houses on the weekends if it meant having gifts under the Christmas tree. We didn't have a lot of money, and by not a lot, I mean barely above the poverty line. My mother was so resourceful. She would find ways to trade her goods and services for my benefit. She would clean a house in exchange for a prom dress. She would volunteer her time in exchange for school uniforms. She box dyed her hair and made things at home. I was truly in awe of how she did it all and never once complained. My mother and I had the closest relationship of any mother-daughter duo that I knew. We relied on each other. We were a team. We loved with all our hearts and also had arguments like brothers and sisters. I had an amazing childhood that was filled with adventure, hard work, and lots and lots of love.

I left home after high school and set out to be the first person in my family to graduate with a college degree. I completed four years with a degree in communications and graduated magna cum laude from Bradley University. I had tons of loans and worked my butt off to finish in the top third of my class. I said goodbye to fairy-tale land and headed off to the real world, or so I thought.

CHAPTER 1

Birthing Life

It took my husband and I a long time to get pregnant with our first child. A long time, meaning seven excruciating months. To someone looking from the outside in, that probably didn't seem like too long of a wait. However, ask the woman who was holding a negative pregnancy test for the sixth month in a row with tears streaming down her face and the look of defeat and failure written all over her body. To her, those six months had been some of the hardest months of her life. She not only questioned herself, her partner, and the entire universe in general, but she also questioned whether she was even fit to be a mother in the first place. She questioned whether this was a sign that she wasn't made to do this. That she wasn't cut out for the role. That everything was against her.

Fast forward to discussing baby number two. I am an only child. My husband came from a family of four boys. We both knew we wanted to have more than one child, and given how long it took us to get pregnant the first time, I thought we needed to start trying fairly soon. God had different plans for us. We found out that we were pregnant with our second child while our first child was only seven months old. Seven months old. It took us seven grueling months to get pregnant with our first child. It wasn't fun or enjoyable. It was a job that ended in heartbreak more times than not. It was work that centered on my body, the times of the month, and an obligation that neither of us looked forward to fulfilling.

The second time around, it took us one time. One time. I literally know the exact hour and day she was conceived because it happened only once that month. When you had a mobile toddler roaming around, it was difficult to schedule alone time with your spouse. Well, it was for me anyway. By the time I was in my bed, any activity other than sleep was completely forbidden. We were chasing a toddler at the time and didn't have a whole lot of time for extracurricular activities, especially those involved once the sun went down.

Our babies were fifteen months a part. We had no idea what we were doing, and for the first two years of parenthood, we were a blur of bottles, diaper changes, sleep deprivation, and repeat. We went from bottles with our first baby to giving those same bottles to our second baby within two months; never once coming up to breathe air. The bottles never got retired for any length of time because they were in a constant rotation. In my opinion, that made all the difference. We didn't have time to recover from one baby. It never got easier for us because we were pulled right back into the trenches. You know that stage where having a toddler starts to get easier as they become more independent? Yeah, we never got to that stage. We stayed in the baby stage for two years with two different babies. To us, that was completely normal because we never knew anything different. It was like the couples who had twins. Everyone wondered how on earth they survived with two babies always needing something at different times. They didn't know any different. They didn't know how else to operate. Two babies had always been their norm. If ignorance were bliss, then we were the happiest parents on the block.

As if birthing a seven-pound nine-ounce human from my vagina and feeling as if my bottom was torn from one hole to the other wasn't enough, I now had to take care of this child. My body felt like I got hit by a truck, ran a marathon, and engaged in a nasty girl fight, and now I had to buckle up and get ready for the Super Bowl. Something was terribly wrong with this picture. I wasn't sure I could safely make it to the bathroom on my own accord without slipping in blood, and now I was responsible for someone else's well-being. And not just keeping said human alive but ensuring he was hitting all the milestones, gaining the appropriate amount of weight at each doctor visit, and being prepared for pre-k. Holy shit! What did I get myself into? At a much later date when my husband was recalling the birth of our firstborn, he described it as a murder scene filled with characters from The Walking Dead. (What a keeper.)

We needed an intermission from delivery to baby. Like, "Hey, wait, this one is still a hot mess and needs more recovery time before we put her in charge of making decisions." You were already starting out at a negative 45% but expected to function at 100%. You know that mom instinct that was supposed to kick in and you would have it all figured out by noon? That wasn't me. I didn't get that high from delivery. I literally had no idea what I was doing, and I didn't trust my delirious self to care for this freshly birthed human.

When I finally got to shower, that was a little piece of heaven on earth. After what seemed like a two-hour process, I put back on my sexy mesh underwear, lined that diaper maxi pad, applied three witch hazel pads, and thought, Oh shit, I forgot the numbing spray; and I started the process all over again. Once this process was finally completed, I had to strategically place the ice back on my vagina to help bring down the swelling and get comfortable. After getting comfortable—there was nothing comfortable about my bottom at this point—the nurses told me that I should get some sleep. They then proceeded to come in every half hour to check on me while bringing me back my child that cried all the time. I thought to myself, Sweet nurse, you're much more equipped to care for this child. Let me know when you want him back. I don't want to hog him. You will only have two days with my sweet child. I will have a lifetime. Soak it in, sister, and please let me sleep.

Nurses are special creatures who are sent from heaven to care for the completely vulnerable, exhausted, just-birthed-a-baby mother. I'm not sure how much nurses get paid, but it is surely not enough. The scene after birth was filled with an excessive amount of fluids, blood, placenta, vomit, diarrhea, emotions, tears, laughter, and an overall state of delirium.

When we finally got our baby home for the first time, we tiptoed around and rarely used the lights because we didn't want to wake up our never-sleeping newborn. Makes perfect sense, right? We believed that if we whispered all the time, maybe, just maybe, our child would figure out how to sleep. Looking back, this was completely ludicrous. We were wrong. For the first three months of my son's life, we would take two-hour shifts while he slept on our chest. We tried seventeen different bottles, and nothing helped. I would nurse, then pump, and then nurse again. It was an endless cycle that gave neither of us any enjoyment. I made up my mind that I was going to breastfeed and I was going to do it whether it killed me. I was too stubborn to recognize that my baby was struggling with latching, I wasn't producing enough milk, and we both were stressed to the max. I felt like a failure if I could not provide the one thing that only a mother could. It was brutal. I was depressed and would sit in the bathroom for hours and cry. I can easily look at the situation now and realize that I was suffering from postpartum depression. When you are in the thick of it, your mind isn't processing information correctly. Instead of looking at the situation for what it truly was, I quickly placed blame on myself for why I was feeling this way. I was the problem. It wasn't situational. It was me.

My son and I never left the house for fear something terrible would happen. Anything could happen in this crazy world out there—traffic, germs, overheating, dehydration, and baby snatchers—but you know how irrational thoughts go.

Once I finally got enough courage to leave the house one day for my six-week postpartum checkup, I was ecstatic. My exciting day trip consisted of visiting my ob-gyn while grabbing a coffee and running to Target. As I strolled up and down the aisles, not really looking for anything in particular, I thought to myself, This is how the rest of the world lives. It was glorious and magical. I came back from my first outing rejuvenated and recharged. I didn't realize how such a small outing could completely change my mood. It was from that point on that I realized I could not stop living because I was responsible for a tiny human. I couldn't lock us away in our house and never leave for fear of having a blown-out diaper, a crying fit, or peeing my pants while trying to find the nearest bathroom. I needed adult human interaction, and he needed to see the world around him. By locking myself and my baby in the house, what was I teaching him?

That the world was a scary place. That it was not safe to leave. That he should live in fear. This wasn't healthy for either of us.

Life is meant to be lived. I didn't want to raise a child who was terrified of the world around him. I wanted him to explore his surroundings, be an adventurous kid, and learn to make his own way in the world. Instead, I was teaching him that the world was a scary place, and we needed to keep our distance. Getting out of the house was a monstrous task because not only did you have to pack four outfit changes, diapers, wipes, bibs, bottles, snacks, a teething necklace, and pacifiers, you also had to remember the thirty-pound car seat and the baby. As if that wasn't enough, you also had to try to make yourself look decent, and by decent I mean no bags under your eyes and five-day-old hair.

Trust me, I know leaving the house is almost not worth it sometimes, but hear me out, Mama. You must leave the house. I repeat. You must leave the house. Even if it takes two hours of preparation and three outfit changes later. You need to be around other people. You need adult conversations. You need a coffee with a friend and a good belly laugh. You need fresh air and a good meal. You must get out of the house. It will rejuvenate you like nothing else can, and the best mama is a happy one.

One of the best pieces of advice I had ever been given about getting the work done came from a coworker I had years ago. He informed me that he actually shit his pants at work one day and went home to change them so he could get back to his job. Let me quote. "Sometimes you stick a tampon up your asshole, and you get back to it." I thought of this statement often when I was struggling with something because it did two things: (1) it made me belly laugh so hard I felt like I was doing a Jillian Michaels: Six-Week Six-Pack workout and (2) it was entirely true.

Things will happen: Your toddler will spill milk on their clothes right before you walk out the door for school. Your child will have an epic meltdown in the aisle of Target because they wanted the multi-colored goldfish instead of the cheddar cheese ones. Your child will poop all over themselves and proceed to smear it on the closest item they can find. Your daughter may want to eat a rice crispy treat for breakfast, and since you forgot to pick up french toast yesterday, you let her. Does that make you a terrible mom for giving your child sugar for breakfast? Heck no. Does that ensure that you will raise an entitled child who thinks she deserves everything? Of course not. It means you are human. There is no way to perfect motherhood. It just isn't able to be perfected. It's messy. It's emotional. It's hard.

You don't have to enjoy every minute of motherhood to be a great mom. You don't have to love the sleepless nights, bottle washing, dirty diapers, never ending snack duties, messy house, piled up laundry, and toddler tantrums. It's 100% acceptable to not love every aspect of motherhood. That doesn't make you a bad mom—it makes you human.

Sometimes you give everything you have and there is nothing left for you to give. But guess what, you're doing the best you can and mama hear me when I say this, it's enough. Your babies love you unconditionally no matter how many times you forget their library book for school. They don't mind how dirty your house is as long as you play a game. They don't care what you make for dinner as long as they have something to eat; even if it is just snacks. They don't care what size dress you wear as long as you give them a hug and a kiss. That's that greatest thing about motherhood-unconditional love.

Somewhere along the way we got the impression that being a great mom means we must love every second of motherhood. We got this idea in our heads that we should feel #blessed all day, every day.

That's not real life. Motherhood isn't perfect images of your family laughing during portraits. Motherhood is asking your son to stop pestering his little sister. Motherhood is getting ready to walk out the door when someone says "I have to poop" after you're already running ten minutes late. Motherhood is consoling your daughter after she loses her favorite unicorn toy. Motherhood is not enjoying every minute of it but knowing that you wouldn't trade it for anything.

Life gets busy. You will forget the breakfast food, and you will want to avoid a drop-down, drag out fight with a stubborn three-year-old at 7:00 a.m. (I'm not sure where she gets that from.) We all need to give ourselves more room for grace. Maybe you're not like me, and you will definitely never dream of giving your child a rice crispy treat for breakfast. Mama, I applaud you. You are killing it. Your planning is admirable. I wish I can be more like you. The point is, things will happen. I can promise you that. Literally thousands and thousands of things will happen, and most of them will be completely out of your control. Expect stuff to happen and you will rarely be disappointed.

Now back to the shitting part. I had an urge to use the bathroom every time I walked into Target. I was not sure if it was the excitement I got from walking by the dollar spot or ten-dollar spot, as it seemed to be these days. Maybe it was the fragrant candles or the overpriced cards. Whatever it was. It happened every damn time. At this stage in my life, I now knew that this was going to happen, and I tried to plan accordingly. Mind you, I had two children that were trying to touch everything in the public restroom, short of licking the toilet lid, and in a fit about why they couldn't get a toy. Then some sweet little old lady shuffled by me in the restroom and said in her sweet grandma voice, "You'll miss it someday." And I gave a half-hearted smile as she exited the restroom. I got it. I really did. I was sure that someday I would miss those little humans who depended on me for everything, but guess what, today was not the day, and tomorrow wasn't looking good either, Shirley. It is completely acceptable to not enjoy every ounce of motherhood without someone much wiser and more experienced telling you otherwise. Like the Florida Georgia Line song "Let it Be," just let it be.

I'm not sure where exactly this fits into my story, but I feel like it is worth noting because it's absolutely ridiculous and completely embarrassing. If you're wondering, it's about shitting. If it helps you feel better about yourself, then my work is done here. The house we brought our babies home from the hospital to started to have sewage problems. It got worse and worse until one day we could no longer use the indoor plumbing we were so accustomed to using. I thought we could just deal with it, but my husband made the executive decision to move to his parents' house fifteen minutes down the road, and I could come back and pack up the necessities we needed for a few days until a plumber could come and fix it. Ironically, a few houses down from us currently had their entire yard torn apart for what I was assuming was a similar situation. After getting the kids settled, I headed back over to our home to collect what I needed. For some reason, when something is unavailable, it becomes a much more sought-after commodity. Like when something says, "do not open" or "do not use," curiosity gets the best of me, and I need to know. On that nice summer afternoon, I was not sure what was in the air, but I had an instant urge that I was going to shit my pants. I knew I couldn't use the toilet, and there was absolutely no way in hell I was going to make it anywhere else. Like the grown thirty-year-old woman that I was, I decided that I could shit in the woods, and no one, not even my husband or father-in-law, who was coming over to try to fix the plumbing, would ever know. So I decided that the embarrassment of actually shitting my pants as an adult woman was worse than shitting in the woods, I chose the latter. I brought my toilet paper with me and found a secluded spot. After wiping and feeling pretty incognito, I left the toilet paper in my business. After packing the rest of the bags, I looked outside again and could see the toilet paper shoved in the pile of shit. I thought to myself, "you dumb ass, animals don't use toilet paper," and my husband would definitely know who did it. I went back out there to the pile of shit and hid the toilet paper under some leaves. I laughed the entire way back to his parents house.

Last shit story. I promise. I went through a stage where I loved making smoothies. Fresh fruit, frozen fruit, vegetables, ginger root, anything, and everything I could find. I had some bananas that were going to go bad, so I froze them. The next week, I decided to put the frozen bananas in the fridge to get somewhat thawed, and when I got home, I planned on whipping out the blender and making something magical. Only, I had a once-in-a-lifetime surprise waiting for me. I had completely forgotten that I put those bananas in the fridge before I left for work that day. My husband, who was a teacher at the time, always got home from work prior to my arrival. I opened the fridge and thought I was going to vomit. The bananas had turned into a mushy brownish concoction that looked exactly like, you guessed it, shit in a bag. I immediately threw it away and started screaming at my husband downstairs about why he would ever shit in a bag and put it in our fridge. Blonde moment maybe? But hey, it was 2019. People can actually send other people flaming bags of poop, so I'm convinced I was just ahead of my time. Birthing life involved an incredible amount of shit. Sometimes children enter the world covered in it. As mothers, sometimes we can't go or we go too much or we have an audience that always has front row rickets to the shit show.

Isn't it absolutely bonkers how busy you thought you were before kids? Like, really, really busy. After all, you had to take care of your own self, your spouse, or your roommate; plus you had to work a full workweek and somehow find time to do laundry, grocery shopping, cleaning, cooking, paying bills, volunteering, parties, and remembering to call your mom at least once a week. I remember thinking, "Man, this adulting stuff is really hard work." How do people make more humans to live with them and still survive? It seems like something only left for the supernatural. How on earth are there enough hours in the day to do everything I currently do and add more responsibilities to my plate? Then once you have a kid, you dream of doing your business alone with no audience and no questions.

And yet by the grace of God, you somehow manage to get it all done. You produce these tiny humans that you will literally give up your own life in exchange for theirs. You feed them, change them, bathe them, love them, and completely adore them. You somehow still manage to bring home a paycheck or stay at home and raise them. You still make it out of the house even if you are perpetually late. At this point in life, you're not quite sure if you would be on time for your own funeral. But that's beside the point. You're doing it, Mama. You're doing it all. The point is, stop dreaming about what your life should look like and appreciate that you have a roof over your head, shit birds to drive you crazy, and friends who are there to drink wine with you when you want to whine about life. By continually wishing for what you want or where your life should be by now, you are robbing yourself of the joy that is in the moment.

You don't have to have it all together to be a great mom. You can serve your child boxed french toast sticks and still be a great mom. You can forget to dress your child in pajamas for pajama day at school and still be a great mom. You can forget to pack your child's lunch and still be a great mom. You can forget to bring treats to school for your child's birthday and still be a great mom. You can forget to brush your child's teeth daily and still be a great mom. Your mistakes don't define your motherhood-your heart does.

I remember looking around one day when my kids were both under two, and I thought, I've made it. I've really made it. I was doing motherhood. I wasn't sure if I was right or not, but I was doing it. I managed to keep them alive, feed them, and still keep some faint resemblance of life before these little rascals arrived. I think it's nothing short of a miracle how this transformation takes place and how we as mamas somehow survive and make it to the other side. You will make it to the other side; I'm living proof.

This season will pass. I promise you it will. I never thought I would ever sleep again after my first son was born. This season you're in is beautiful and hectic and magical. But it will pass. Things will get easier. Time will march on, and someday you will blink and wonder how they got so old. You will look back at old pictures and reminisce about those times. They went from toddlers who threw tantrums over everything to spending the night with their friends and going to their room to play by themselves. They went from needing me to do absolutely everything to playing on sport teams and reading books on their own. Seasons that I thought would never pass did and looking back they passed quicker than I could have ever imagined. This is the part that no mom is ever fully prepared to digest. The idea that your children are growing up. They are exploring the world around them, going on adventures and learning more and more every day of their lives. There isn't a book that can prepare you for that transition. Those days you thought would never end and the nights that seemed to drag on for eternity are now gone. You will rekindle your friendships with those that you lost touch with in those early years of motherhood. You will start to pick up hobbies that you used to enjoy. You will have an occasional date night. You will start to get back to some version of yourself. You will never truly be who you were pre-kids. Too much has happened. Too many things were experienced.

But you will become a new you. A better you, a wiser and more experienced you. A person who has compassion and understanding and has a love so deep it can move mountains.

CHAPTER 2

Falling Means You Get Another Chance

When I was a junior in high school, my amazing track coach told me that he thought I would be really great at running hurdles. I had never before in my life ran over a stationary object while running and was somewhat perplexed as to why he believed I would excel at this task. I negligently agreed only because our current hurdler was injured and there were only so many positions to fill at a track meet.

He was so incredibly right. I ended up placing first, second, or third in almost all my races, including the one hundred high hurdles and the three hundred low hurdles. I ended up qualifying for sectionals my senior year, where I was placed in lane four. Everyone who runs knows what lane four means. For the rest of you, it means that I was the fastest runner in my heat and should place first, given my prior running times. Considering this was the meet where you qualify for state, I was destined for the state track. I feel like it is important to note that I went to a Catholic high school in a small town where our track shirt stated, "We don't think we are better than you. It's the IHSA that thinks we are 65 percent better than you." This meant that at a private school, they would multiply our enrollment by .65 to make the competition fair when we were competing against a public school. We had a long line of successful runners and plenty of state medals and accolades to show for it. The state meet was a place our team made home and every runner couldn't wait to get their ticket. Going into this meet, I was confident that I would qualify for state. I was even envisioning my awesome uniform at state and how I would do my hair for the meet, which socks would be my lucky ones, and so on. When I shot out of the blocks on my one-hundred-meter hurdle, it started like any other race. I was so far ahead of all the other runners that I had nothing to worry about. Then, to my dismay, a runner out of the left corner of my eye started to gain on me. This was the first time during the entire year that I felt someone closing the gap on me, and I panicked. I tried to go faster, but when you were running over stationary objects that I was talking about, you could only gain so much speed without falling flat on your face. My left foot crossed the right lane as I was trying to push my body across the finish line. The cameras caught this, and there was a review set up for the finish. When a runner intervened with another runner's lane, they were automatically disqualified, regardless of whether they interfered with the runner's ability to finish the race.

As I set my blocks for the three-hundred-meter low hurdles, I awaited my fate from the first race. I was visibly upset about what happened, and two minutes before the race started, the young girl holding the blocks on my team told me that my lane interference caused me to be disqualified from the one-hundred-meter hurdles. I was beyond devastated. Moments later, I was supposed to pull myself together, knowing that this was the only race I could win to qualify for the state meet. When the gun went off, I was absolutely terrified. Terrified that I wouldn't win and let my coach down; upset for the silly mistake I made during the first race and how I let my hard work go down the drain if I couldn't win a blue medal in this one. My emotions got the best of me, and my left knee clipped the first hurdle, and I fell to the ground. My coach and all my teammates knew the impact of this fall, but there was one person who didn't—me. I instantly got back up and tried my damnedest to beat those other runners. I didn't know if it was emotion or adrenaline or what, but I almost caught up to them. But almost only counts in horseshoes. By the time I crossed the finish line, I was bawling with despair and my knees were covered in blood. My entire track career built up to this moment, and I totally blew it. I disappointed my coach, my teammates, and most importantly, myself. All that hard work, sweat, and tears for what? I thought.

It was only years later that I truly understood the victorious feats I had accomplished that day. You see, what I thought was my greatest failure actually became my greatest accomplishment. It wasn't courageous that I started the race; it was courageous that I finished. It wasn't about how I should have won the race and went on to state only to get completely left in the dust by the much faster runners; it was the fact that I was brave enough to get myself off that tire track and finish the race. Later, my teammates told me that they would have just faked an injury or rolled off the track to avoid the public humiliation that ensued. The odd thing was, that never even crossed my mind. I never thought for one second that I would quit just because I fell on the first hurdle. If these runners were going to beat me, they would have to do it at the last hurdle.

I wanted to go down in history at my high school for being an outstanding runner and hurdler. I wanted my name plastered all over the walls to show the awards and the medals that I received along the way. Instead, I was going to be known as the girl whose track season ended much too early. The girl whose nerves got the best of her when she competed against real competition. The girl who just didn't have it in her to make it to the state meet with the big dogs. Part of me still wishes I won that race. There is part of me that wants to have had the experience to compete at such a pristine level, but I'll never have that chance. There were bigger lessons for me to learn that day. In fact, I barely remember all the first-place medals or plaques I received from running hurdles that year. At eighteen years old, I believe that falling on that track taught me more than receiving a first place medal at sectionals.

I kept in touch with my track coach and still do to this day. He told me several years ago that one of his favorite stories is about me—my senior year at sectionals. He proceeded to tell me that he tells every track team he has had since then about my story. "She never hesitated. She never blinked. She never thought for a second that she still didn't have a chance to win that race. She fought till the very end, and that makes her a winner."

I hold that story dear to my heart because it makes me human for losing the race yet shows how resilient my spirit is for never quitting. Rolling off the track and faking an injury would have been the easy way out. Making up some story about how my hamstring got knotted up would have been the path of least resistance. The easy path never crossed my mind. True winners work hard until the very end. True winners get tough when things get hard. True winners don't look around for excuses; they look for motivation. You should be proud of what you have accomplished and how far you've come regardless of what anyone else has to say about it. They don't define you. Only you can define you.

They can't beat you if you don't quit. Isn't that what they say? One day I got fired, rehired, and told my boss to go to hell. My day job was working for a family agriculture business where my father-in-law was my boss, and I worked with my husband. Not the easiest setup in the world. But that was not what this particular story was about. Needless to say, there were many open sores, hard feelings, and downright turmoil for years to come following my husband's decision to leave the company. The entire reason we moved was for this business—I was left having my father-in-law as my boss. This left me in an impossible situation. One that I wasn't truly prepared to handle. I had my husband's feelings that I needed to handle with care but also remaining professional in my current business role. The only thought I had at the time was that I needed to keep my job since my husband just left his, and both of us living on love just wasn't going to work.

I had a duty that I gave my husband when we said our vows and that was for better or worse; no matter what. It wasn't for better or for worse when it was convenient. It wasn't for better or for worse when things were in complete order, and it sure as shit wasn't for better or for worse when the world was spinning on its perfect axis. That vow meant that when shit was hitting the fan, and the world was coming to a screeching halt, that you would still support one another. It wasn't my decision to make. It was his. His happiness was more important than any corporate job. If you couldn't work happy, then what were you really doing?

Did you know that when Rosa Parks was interviewed about giving her seat up on the bus, she said she didn't even think about it? It wasn't a premeditated delivery. She didn't create an action plan for how she was going to change the world. She simply refused to give up her seat on the bus because she was tired of standing. She believed that she had every right that the white people had to sit on that bus. She reacted to the situation. No game plan. No direction. Simply action.

I didn't know what would happen on that fateful day when I entered the office after the shit was still hanging on the fans. I didn't plan my strategy or decide what I would say if this or that happened. It just happened. I got to the office on Monday morning, and when my boss (remember he happened to be my father-in-law) said, "Good morning," I simply shrugged my shoulders. I didn't have anything to say, and honestly, I was emotionally drained from the aftermath of what happened last week.

My boss continued again with the words "I said good morning."

I responded with "I don't have anything to say."

He got up from his chair and fired me right on the spot. He told me to collect my things and get out. I had never been fired once in my entire existence, and I had only been dumped once by a boyfriend, which was probably why that one hurt so bad. I wasn't used to being told no, and I definitely was not used to being fired. I looked him square in the eye and said, "No, I will not leave. I have farmers that I need to talk with today."

Then one thing led to another, and it turned into a full-on episode of Jerry Springer equipped with multiple threats, lots of cussing, and the cops almost being called. My boss literally just fired me, and I told him to take a walk because I had work that I needed to get done. Who in their right mind does that? Who gets fired, calls their boss's bluff, and continues on with the job they just got fired from? Me. That's who. Someone who is completely out of their mind. Someone who doesn't quit until they get the job done. Someone who takes zero shits, and someone who knows when someone is bluffing.

Looking back, I never planned on doing what I did. It literally just happened. The words were out of my mouth before I could even really process what I just said. I told my boss that he couldn't fire me. I told him that I would not walk out the door because I had people, lots of people, counting on me. I wasn't going to let him win. I wasn't going to fold like a cheap lawn chair after everything that I had put into this business. It simply wasn't going to happen. No one was going to tell me what I was or wasn't capable of—even if that person happened to be my boss.

To this day, my best friend tells me that I am the only person on the planet that would get fired from a job and continue working on the work she just got fired from doing. I didn't plan on going into work that day and being fired, keeping my job, and then getting rehired, but that was exactly what happened. Sometimes we don't need a detailed plan with eighteen bullet points for every move we make in life. Don't get me wrong. I love a good Sharpie-colored, detailed calendar just like all you other type A personalities out there, but sometimes the best decisions we make are the ones we don't plan out. They are the decisions that get made with our heart instead of our head. The gut reaction instead of the thoughtful itinerary, and the faith instead of the reason. Sometimes the overthinking and over-indulging only creates more fog when we are just trying to see out the windshield.

They say hindsight is twenty-twenty. I could have packed up my desk and walked out that door for the very last time. I decided there was more in my career that had yet to be written, and I was not going to have anyone, including my boss, take that away. Don't let anyone tell you when the door will be shut. Don't let anyone tell you you're not educated enough or pretty enough or experienced enough to make the next move. And especially don't settle for anything that you didn't decide for yourself. At the end of the day, your decisions are a reflection of you and no one else. There is no phone a friend in life. It's you and only you. You get to choose the life you want to live.

I am no psychologist, so I'm not sure how this actually plays out in the human mind, but why do we relentlessly obsess about our failures yet never take time to celebrate our triumphs? You can win ten medals for competing in races, yet the one you lose sticks out in your head. You can have three hundred great parenting moments throughout the day, but you'll only remember the one where you completely lost it with your kids after asking them to pick up their toys for the hundredth time. You can be the best karaoke queen of your town or the best baker or the best writer or the best coach, but you will always remember those times when you fall short. That doesn't make you a failure. It makes you human. The only way you really fail is if you stay down and don't get back up.

I used to go through my entire day questioning everything I did as a parent. Did I allow my child too much screen time today? Was their diet adequate enough to help them reach their full potential? Did they get a solid nap? Did I review sight words and numbers today? Was everything I was doing setting them up for disaster? Let's cut to the spoiler alert. You will fail at times as a mother. You will lose your cool and go off on your child. Your patience will wear thin after the tenth time you have asked them to stop doing something. You will forget to pack lunch, sign the papers, clean all the uniforms, get their haircut, forget their favorite stuffed animal, forget about the fundraiser, and the list goes on. But guess what, you will always be the best mom in their eyes. They don't want a perfect mom; they want their mom. They don't judge you for the dinners you cook or whether or not you're on time for school. Your entire existence as a mother isn't dependent on whether you packed their library book for school. They don't hold a grudge when you get upset with them. They aren't mad that they have to wear a somewhat dirty uniform to the game. They love unconditionally. Your failures don't define your motherhood. Your failures are lessons, and without lessons, we fail to learn. You are a better person for your failures. They teach you a lesson. Sometimes they aren't a pleasant lesson but a lesson nonetheless. You are a stronger person for failing and trying again than you ever would have been if you simply succeeded the first time around.

You will fail at being a mother. You will fail at being a spouse. You will fail at being a friend. You will fail at being a daughter. And every single time you fail, you will be made whole again. You have the choice to decide what you want to do with that failure. Failure decides how tough you really are. Failure decides how driven you are to get back up from your hardships. Failure is what separates the good from the great. You have the power to choose your destiny. Your story isn't meant to end with a failure. Flip that failure into your greatest accomplishment yet.

No one ever looks back on their life and thinks, Man, I tried way too many things in my life. They may regret the things they didn't do but never the other way around. If you're too afraid to take the first step, how are you ever going to know if you can climb the mountain?

Failing means you get another chance. Failing means you're still breathing. Failing means you still have a fight left in you. So get up, brush off your knees, and keep running in the direction of your dreams. You're going to learn so much more from your failures than you ever will from your successes. Your failures teach you to dig deeper, try harder, and push further. Success teaches you to be content with what you have. Being content means you aren't growing. Choose to grow.

CHAPTER 3

Find Your Village

It was 3:44 p.m. when I got a call from my children's school. I instantly panicked and tried to find them in the house to ensure I picked them up from school today. Yep, they are here. Oh no, did I forget to pay the tuition? I was certain that I did. I reluctantly answered. It was the school secretary, and like the good little Catholic girl that I am, I braced myself for the reprimand. She first told me to "hear her out" before I said no. No good conversation started with that, and I was instantly defensive. I kept thinking, land the damn plane so I can say no, lady. She then asked me if I would be the head track coach for grades kindergarten through third. This would entail having three local Catholic schools form a team. She might have well asked me if I would be willing to run for mayor of the town. I was so ecstatic and excited, but I thought the mature response would be to say, "Let me discuss this with my husband first." Deep down I knew I didn't care what he said; I was going to be the head coach. This was a dream that I had always had, and I couldn't believe that this opportunity presented itself. I wasn't about to let anyone squash my dreams of having the name coach printed on the back of my t-shirt. The school wanted me to lead these precious kids. They wanted me to teach them skills and run drills and be a part of something bigger than myself. The excitement I felt was indescribable.

Before I continue, let me say that I truly have the best friends. I know that gets thrown around a lot, but guys, it's true. I know they will be there in a second if I need it, and we laugh until our bellies hurt. They are my girls. My tribe and I cannot imagine going through life without them.

I then started to quickly tell my mom and any friend that would listen. However, when I began telling my close friends about it, I kept catching myself saying things like "I know it's totally silly" and "I don't know why I am so excited" and "How funny that I said I would do this" and so on. I was playing small. I felt the need to downplay my enthusiasm because I didn't know how they would respond. I was changing my behavior based on how I presumed others would take it. I was convinced they were going to make fun of me or laugh at how silly the situation appeared. Looking back, I cannot believe that I felt that way. These were my closest friends, and of course they were going to support me and celebrate with me. But just because it wasn't their dream, I thought they might giggle at mine. Own your dream. Don't downplay it or push it aside or hide it because of what other people may think. If you don't fully believe in your dream, why should they? It's your life and your dreams, and no one is going to care about it more than you. Your peers may have their own dreams that they have been frightened to share for fear of what you may think. So stop hiding it in the closet. Stop letting your fears control your behaviors. Not only did my village support me they made me Coach Hendrix shirts and bought me whistles, cones, and stopwatches. They even offered to help me coach if I needed more assistance for twenty-three kids under eight years of age. Your true village will be there to support you in any endeavor, and if they aren't, then find a new village; there's plenty out there.

Before the first track practice, I was terrified. What had I gotten myself into? What if the parents started having suggestions about how I should be doing things? What if they thought Bobby should be running faster or Susie needed more time working on her baton hand offs? What if the kids didn't like me? After day one, that all quickly went by the wayside. Remember, I was volun-told, not volunteered, for this position. The kids were fantastic, the parents supportive, and most importantly, everyone was having fun.

Isn't is crazy how we tend to borrow trouble? Instead of going into a situation with positive vibes and good intentions, we spend most of our brainpower focusing on creating problems that don't even exist. I believe that positive people create positive environments. Negative people surround themselves with people who are equally as miserable. Instead of borrowing trouble and focusing on everything negative that can happen, we should be using all that energy into focusing on something positive. Imagine how further along we will be if we focus more on our positive energy.

Finding your village is so vital to your success of becoming the best version of yourself. Some people are put on this earth to inspire you and push you to do more; others are put on this earth to literally suck your soul dry. Choose wisely. Which village you decide to associate with will either help or hinder your success. The older I get, the more I realize that I need a core group of friends to complete my village. Quality over quantity is key.

It was May 8th, 2019. I picked up the kids from school and decided we would go to the park until my mother-in-law picked them up for a sleepover. I sent out a text message to every friend I had within ten miles to see if anyone was available for a drink or three. Everyone was busy with dance practice, dinner plans, work, and just plain exhaustion. I decided to go for a run and had this crazy idea to try to run farther than I ever had before. I turned on my audiobook to The Five-Second Rule by Mel Robbins and got after it. Absolutely incredible book, and I highly recommend you either listen or read it. She gives simple yet groundbreaking advice on how to get out of your head and on with your life. Okay, back to the running part. Prior to May 8th, 2019, the longest run I ever completed was six miles. Something about that six-mile mark that I just couldn't make my legs move anymore. I honestly thought that would be the farthest I would ever be able to run. I think the reason I wasn't able to run longer than six miles was because it was in my head that I couldn't. Physically, there was nothing different I did on May 7th, when I only ran two miles, as opposed to May 8th, where I ran ten miles. Ten miles. I ran ten freaking miles. The difference was that instead of telling myself I couldn't do it, I told myself that I could. Every time that negative self-talk would start to rise up, I would smash it with "Five, four, three, two, one" (Thanks, Mel Robbins). Instead of doubting myself and questioning whether I had it in me or not, I kept telling myself, "Just one more mile. Just one more."

Like a lot of things in life, running is much more mind over matter. If we can control our thoughts, we can control our actions. If we can control our actions, we can change our lives. The mental games we play in our head all day can have a negative impact on our overall happiness and ability to crush our goals. My ability to run ten miles instead of two had absolutely nothing to do with my physical abilities. It was my brain that told me it wasn't possible. It was my negative self-talk that kept ruining my ability to keep going and get to the ten-mile mark.

Do you know how many times a day I doubt myself? A ton. I go through my entire day pretty much questioning everything from my work to my parenting to a goal I say I want to achieve to something I want to accomplish. I question it all over and over and over again. Can I really do that? Why do I think I should? Is it even possible? How long will it take? Will I have the time? Am I really capable? The negative voice in my head tells me how incapable and incompetent I am daily.

I have to become louder and more powerful than the negative self-talk. I have to be stronger, driven, and optimistic. When I was training for my marathon, I would catch myself when those negative thoughts would creep into my head. I would literally have to tell myself, "No, Jen. Not today. We don't have time to question whether or not you can or should do this. We are way too invested at this point. It's happening whether you think it should or not."

You and I are capable of so much more than we think. You have the ability to do anything that you put your mind to. First, you just need to get out of your head and on with your life. We all know that I am no expert. I am in no position to guide you on this crazy thing called life. All I'm telling you is that I think we can do a lot more with our lives and achieve larger goals if we stop telling ourselves that we can't. If we treat ourselves the way we treat our children, our partner, our family, or our friends, we will likely be much happier and have a fighting chance at achieving our goals in life. We would never talk negatively to those people we love, but we have no problem running ourselves into the ground all day long. I read somewhere that we have anywhere from 12,000 to 60,000 thoughts that go through our heads per day. Per day. Guess what percentage of those thoughts are negative. Eighty percent. That means that well over half of our day is consumed with negative thoughts about ourselves, our life, others, our work, our kids, and so on. Imagine how unstoppable we will be if eighty percent of our thoughts per day are positive.

Your mind's purpose is to keep you safe from danger. Its purpose is to help you play it safe and stay away from danger. For example, I can cross the street, but I better check for traffic first. I can quit my nine-to-five and start my own business, but what if it fails? I can run a ten-kilometer race, but what if I don't finish? What if? What if you fail? How will you ever know if you can do it unless you try? At least you will know one hundred percent whether it will have worked or not, and you don't have to spend the rest of your life wondering what if. Failing doesn't mean that your life is over. Failing means you can now go in the same direction you are going with more wisdom or choose to go in a different direction.

Your mind can literally talk you out of anything. The second you have an idea for something, within seconds, the rational part of your brain begins to question your thoughts. What if this happens? What if that happens? You can talk yourself out of anything if you start to let your mind wander. Your brain is logical, whereas your heart relies on emotion. The feelings of your heart don't always make sense. Why you choose to fall in love with certain people, the ideas you have for your career, your desire to travel or to have a hobby. We can't always explain why our heart feels a certain way. Our brains try to keep us logical and lucid, whereas our hearts are irrational and illogical. That doesn't make the brain superior over the heart; they bother serve two entirely different functions in our lives.

What the mind does not understand, the heart already knows. If you let your brain talk you out of your dreams, you'll never accomplish them. It's harsh but it's true. I don't care how deeply that dream or idea is on your heart; if you let your head talk you out of it, it will never happen. If you let other people dictate how you live your life, you will forever be their slave. If you don't take the plunge and jump right in headfirst with everything on the line, it won't happen. Your heart has known what it truly wants this whole time. Who you are as a person and what brings you joy in life and lights your on soul fire has always been present. It's your head that's holding you back.

We always wait for the perfect time to do something; whether it's to start eating healthier, sign up for that race, ask for that promotion, go out on a date, start the new business that we have always dreamed of, go to the concert, or write the book. If having children has taught me anything, it's that there is no perfect time. There will never be a perfect time. The time is now. You're never going to do it if you don't just dive in. If you let yourself get used to the cold pool water, it's never going to happen. You have to dive in headfirst and get it over with. The confidence you will gain from having the courage to do it will transform your life. The outcome is not important. What is important is that you have the courage to try in the first place. Who cares if your book is not a New York Times best seller? Who cares if the boy says no to a date? Who cares if you don't run the time you want for the race? It does not matter. You need to get out of your head and into your heart. Your true passions will light your soul on fire. What's worse than getting to the end of your life and not having completed your goals? Not even trying—that's what's worse. Leaving those what-ifs to chance. Only when you try it and do it will you figure out whether you are made to do it. I don't know about you, but I don't want to get to the end of my life and wish I would have done the things that are on my bucket list. Your dreams and aspirations are on your heart for a reason. You are capable of more than you think. You have unique gifts to offer the world that are waiting to be revealed. You just have to have enough courage to act upon them.

I have always been a sucker for togetherness. I love getting groups of people together to work toward a common goal. Whether that goal is to win a track meet, finish a group project, a wedding, or have a birthday. I am a people person, and I get energized being around others. My husband, on the other hand, is completely an introvert. He prefers quite time and is actually one of those psychopaths that enjoys his own company. WTF? I'm always, like, "Don't you get lonely? or bored? or wonder if you're still alive with the rest of society?" Nope. He loves it. So paying money to be in a race of agony and pain and around tons of people who are super hyped up about the goal they are working towards isn't his idea of Sunday Funday.

I was a little skeptical about even taking him with me for my first half marathon because what if it didn't go so well? I wanted to, correction, needed to have someone with me just in case something happened and I ended up in the hospital.

If you know anything about runners, they are a different breed. They have to be, right? Who voluntarily signs up and pays money to run a race and push their body to the absolute max? They are dedicated like no other. They run in rain, sleet, extreme hot, and extreme cold; and they do it while building others up along the way. They wait in long Porta Potty lines to nervous-shit their brains out before the gun goes off. They blow their nose like snot rockets on the sidewalk and pee their pants along the way. They develop sweat in places on their body they didn't know could sweat. They lose toenails, gel packets, and water bottles along the way.

I absolutely love the camaraderie that takes place on race day. Spouses cheering on spouses, friends, grandparents, fiancés, college students, and kids who are all there to support their super man or woman. There are super young kids all the way up to individuals in their eighties who I admire deeply. Anyone can run, but it takes dedication and training to do it well. It's about people coming together from all walks of life, all running for different reasons. Some do it because they have a love for running. Others do it because they want the accomplishment that goes with crossing the finish line. Others run to show their kids how important physical fitness is, and others run for the thrill.

I love running because running knows no age. It doesn't discriminate based on age, sex, religion, or background. You don't need fancy gym equipment or a pricey membership to run. You don't need anything but a pair of gym shorts and tennis shoes. Running is a resource that is available to everyone, everywhere. Running is a sport that can carry you through the years after you no longer engage in softball league, basketball, or wiffleball. It truly is a lifelong sport. That's why I love it.

Running gives me goose bumps. There is something about participating in something that is larger than myself that makes me feel alive.

I wanted to complete 13.1 miles. In my mind, I wanted to be among the elite runners and be able to say, "Yep, I did it." It became a goal that I wanted to achieve in 2019. My friends, family, and spouse thought I was absolutely insane. I couldn't even find anyone to train with me let alone actually run the half marathon. I realized that it was okay that no one wanted to run the race. After all, it wasn't their dream they were chasing, it was mine. I wanted it. Would I have loved having a partner to train with? Hell yes! But was it completely necessary? No. I had to be my own motivation. I had to schedule the workouts, get the miles in, drink enough water, eat right, stay motivated, and keep going. I'm not gonna lie. It was tough. With so many other things begging for my attention—from kids, to work, to groceries, to laundry, and everything in between—it felt overwhelming. There were many times where I thought I bit off more than I could chew.

What made the difference in my mind was the fact that I had a great support system. I had friends that had no problem watching my kids for an hour while I went for a run. I had grandparents that took the kids for sleepovers so I could train. I had a husband that never complained about my running once because he knew how bad I wanted to accomplish this goal. You can't do it all on your own all of the time. People have nannies and housekeepers and grocery shoppers and babysitters. There is no way you can do everything on your own. It's one hundred percent impossible, and you're going to burn your stick at both ends if you try. Then not only will you have zero energy to work on your goals, but you'll also have zero energy to show up for your kids, spouse, work, and everything else. My family and friends earned that medal just as much as I did. Without their support, it would never have been possible. It's okay to ask for help. It's completely acceptable to rely on other people sometimes. I believe that the more you give, the more you get back. Do you think that I'll be willing to help out those friends and family members when they need it? You bet. They helped me reach a lifelong goal of mine, and I am forever indebted to them.

We had a song we sang in Girl Scouts that was called "Make New Friends." The lyrics said, "Make new friends, but keep the old. One is silver, and the other is gold." I think it's important to find new friends wherever you live. Some of them may not measure up to your golden friends, but so what? Trust me when I tell you this; you will be such a happier mother, wife, and person once you find your village. I have some friends that I keep in touch with that I have known for most of life. However, I think it is so important to your overall well-being to have a few friends to meet for cocktails or lunch, go on a shopping trip, or drop the kids off for a playdate when you need some sanity. It's not the same as talking on the phone with your golden friends. You need personal interaction. You need to share laughs and stories and make memories. You need playdates and outings and birthday parties. Once I found my village, my adult life changed. Believe me when I tell you, it's vital.

I never really understood the domino effect and how one change in behavior can cause other changes in different areas of your life. After I ran my half marathon, I felt unstoppable. It improved my relationship with my husband for the amount of support and encouragement he provided throughout the process. Watching him support me on the course that day made me feel so grateful, loved, and appreciated. After that race, I felt like we could move mountains. It makes me want to show up for him to reciprocate the support I felt while I was working to accomplish my goal. His goals and aspirations are just as important as mine, and if we work together as a team to build one another up, we both win. To me, that is the very essence of marriage. After I placed fifty-ninth overall female in the half marathon and finished in two hours and twelve minutes, I felt like I could accomplish anything. If I was willing to put in the work, I could achieve it. See, finishing that half marathon did three things. First, it increased my own self-worth. Second, it brought me closer to my husband. Third, it gave me the push I needed to finish writing this book. That one event created a domino effect in all these other areas of my life. Don't get me wrong; it was hard as hell. There were times during the race where I didn't know if I could make it to the end. But your body and mind are capable of so much more than you think. My mental endurance had to be stronger than my physical limitations. You can do anything you set your mind to.

Like the Ja Rule song "Mesmerize," "Every woman just wanna be happy." That's what we all want. We all want to feel accepted at work, with our friendships, our spouses, our children, and our family. The older I get, the more I realize the things that are truly important. I don't worry about the materialist things that I thought would bring me joy or the trivial things in life. The things that are important to me now are things that money can't buy. When I was younger, I thought if I only got this job or that car, I would be happy. If only my spouse would take out the trash without being asked, I would be happy. If only I had the best makeup, a boob lift, or lipo-suction, I would then experience true happiness. Well, guess what, ladies. It doesn't. If you want to get a boob job, go do it. If you want those Louis Vuitton shoes and you have the money, then go get them, girl. But don't think for one second that it will bring you last-ing happiness. It won't. Everything in this world is fleeting, and once you get one thing that you want, there will always be something new on the market that will catch your eye and become a must-have. This continuous cycle will never end. Trust me; I have tried it.

In my adult life, I had never had to live paycheck to paycheck or hope that there was enough money in the bank when I swiped my debit card for groceries. My husband came from a family that did very well for themselves. They worked hard and understood how to make their money make more money. They had savings accounts and 401(k)s and mutual funds and emergency savings, and they planned for their future. When I got married, I felt financially secure. My husband knew what he was doing and set us up for success. I loved being able to swipe that credit card without any worries. In fact, I got a little too comfortable swiping. It wasn't until my husband realized that his current job wasn't for him and decided to pursue a different avenue that I began thinking differently about money. For the first time since my childhood, we didn't have a surplus of money. It was a pivotal moment in my adult life as I realized the true meaning of the dollar bill. Sure, I remember pinching pennies when I was younger, but that seemed like a lifetime ago. Working all those extra jobs and paying bills and taking out loans to try to make it all work. That was then; this is now.

The things that will bring you true happiness in this life are the long-term goals that you are working toward. No one ever says, "Man, I wish I wouldn't have tried to write that book" or "I wish I would have never ran this half marathon" or "I wish I would have never pursued those goals at work to better my career." We all have items on our bucket list. Those things that we long to do before our days come to an end. Just because you are a mother does not mean that you have to give up on your life long goals. You are a better mother and a better person for going after your dreams and crushing your goals. Your entire existence should not be made up of cooking and cleaning. Don't use the "I'm tired" excuse to hold off on your dreams. You aren't tired; you're uninspired.

You have to get out of survival mode. Surviving isn't living. It's merely waiting for the hours to pass until you can be done with your life. Choose to thrive, not survive. Your gifts are too precious to be wasted on your unwillingness to use them. Your life and your heart will be lit on fire once you find what you are made to do.

After running the half marathon, I was hungry for more or "thirsty," as the young kids say today. If I could run 13.1 miles, maybe I could run 26.2 miles. If I could put in the rigorous training and commitment, maybe I could achieve the impossible. We are always going to think we can't do something, until we do. The training for a marathon was long; the summer was hot and humid, and having two small children competing for my time and attention made the task difficult. I didn't want to give up on myself. I didn't want to feel guilty for taking this time to work on achieving my goal. I didn't want to spend the rest of my life thinking what if I would have done it? What if I could have achieved what so few people have?

During my training, I only got up to fourteen miles. All the marathon training guides I read encouraged a mileage of eighteen to twenty miles in order to be ready for race day. I was running consistently, but the longer runs were difficult for me to accomplish. I questioned myself over and over again about whether or not I had it in me to complete the 26.2 miles. I had it all along. My perseverance, work ethic, and dedication had been there all along. I finished the marathon in five hours and thirty-four minutes. There were times where I had out-of-body experiences. I wasn't sure if I was running or I was watching myself compete. There were times I didn't know if I would ever make it to the finish line. There were times I closed my eyes and placed myself somewhere else so I wouldn't think about the pain.

It's hard to put into words the feelings and emotions that were wrapped up in that day. From the friends that came to cheer me on to the other friends that put on their running shoes and supported me along the course, to the balloons, flowers, gifts, and signs along the way; it was nothing short of magical. The love and support from my friends and family carried me through the finish line. My medal was for all of us to share. My village deserved the medal just as much as I did. There are no words to describe the feeling of turning the last corner and seeing the finish line within reach. The hours spent training, the sweat poured out, the sore feet and legs, the blood, and the tears all came together for one glorious moment in time. I will never forget how I felt crossing that finish line for as long as I live.

Here are ten things I learned during my marathon:

We are capable of so much more than we have ever imagined.
Cheering each other on is how we will all go far in life.
Overcoming hardship is mind over matter.
Perseverance is key in all we do.
With great hardship comes great reward.
Mentors are the building blocks to the mountains we want to climb.
Never underestimate the people you meet along the way.
Regardless of pain, keep putting one foot in front of the other.
Relish in the moments that take your breath away.

Never forget how hard you have worked and how much you have accomplished.

Doing hard things in life changes our ability to do other hard things. I went from questioning whether I had it in me to complete 26.2 miles to "Yes, I ran a marathon." I went from wondering if I bit off more than I could chew to completing one of the greatest challenges of my life. We always think we can't do something until we do. Until we prove to ourselves that we are strong enough, smart enough, and capable enough. And guess what; you are enough.

Once you complete something hard, you can draw on that experience in every other aspect of your life. I always come back to my marathon when I am questioning my ability to do something. If I can run 26.2 miles, I can write a book. If I can complete a marathon, I can place first overall female in a 5K race. If I can do one of the hardest things of my life, I totally got this thing called motherhood. As scary as it seems sometimes, I got this.

Once you complete one task, it will help you snowball that next hurdle you want to scale or mountain you want to climb. With each task you accomplish, you will gain more confidence for the next one, and before you know it, you'll start believing in yourself like you never have before. It's always better to try something new and fail than to stay in mediocrity. You will learn so much about yourself from trying something new and failing than you ever will from staying on the beaten path. Finding your village is like having a group of girls in the boxing ring who are rooting for you, providing you with hydration and putting bandages on your hands when you get hurt. They breath life into you and make you believe that anything is possible.

CHAPTER 4

Use Your Strengths

If it isn't a "hell yeah," then it's probably a "hell no." Go with your gut. If you aren't super stoked about marrying the person you're with, then something probably isn't right. If you aren't ready to move across the country, what is holding you back? If you don't think you're ready to go back to school, change jobs, leave toxic friends, or visit your crazy family for the holidays, then don't. Whenever I am questioning whether or not to do something and I'm not one hundred percent into it, why half-ass it? Saying yes to something I don't want to do, takes away from the things I do have a passion to pursue. As a wife, mother, daughter, friend, and coworker, my time is precious, and what I decide to do with it is completely my decision. I don't have time to waste on people, places, activities, trips, or anything else that doesn't serve a meaningful purpose. The more I build my life around the things that bring me happiness, the closer I get to living my best life. My best life isn't going to be the same as yours. You may love CrossFit, art, museums, orchestras, plays, or festivals. Whatever it is that you love, fill your life with more of it; lots more.

We all have things we do well and things we don't. I can run a mean 5K race, but being crafty with my children's valentines for school, eh, not so much. I tend to stick with the premade sticker valentines. I love to plan out my meals, week, month, and even year, but sometimes I forget to live in the moment and appreciate the small things. I can plan a killer kid's birthday party but struggle with being patient in everyday life. I took the StrengthsFinder assessment when I was a junior in college at Bradley University. Go Braves! I minored in leadership studies, and this course was centered around working from our strengths. The premise of the book is that you cannot be anything you want to be, but you can become a lot more of who you already are. We have a greater potential for success if we build upon what we already excel at instead of trying to fix areas where we struggle. We have innate strengths that are apparent from a very young age, and if we learn to develop those strengths, over time they will help us flourish into the person we are meant to become. After you take the thirty-minute assessment, you get your top five strengths. My top five strengths are achiever, discipline, competition, relator, and futuristic. The goal of this chapter is to figure out what you do well and capitalize on it in both life and motherhood.

Let's start with achiever. An achiever personality "works hard and possess a great deal of stamina. They take immense satisfaction in being busy and productive" (Strengths Finder 2.0). If you have ever read the book to your children called How to Fill a Bucket by Carol McCloud, this sums up the achiever perfectly. I have this bucket with me every day, and in order to feel satisfied with myself, I have to complete a certain amount of tasks in order to fill my bucket. This can be anything from working my day job, to emptying the dishwasher, to folding laundry, to running, or getting birthday gifts ready for the party next weekend. I always have to stay busy. You'll never catch me lying on the couch watching a show because I can think of one million other things I can be doing. It is even difficult for me to go on vacation and just relax with a book because it isn't checking off anything on my ever-growing to-do list. This strength can be a positive attribute in motherhood because I am always on the go, always thinking of the next thing that is coming up and making sure I am prepared. By using this strength to my advantage, I am continually in a forward motion with my children, which works out well since they never stop moving either. If this sounds like you, find a way to capitalize on this strength and use it to your advantage. Teach your children to help with putting away laundry, cleaning dishes, and organizing their toys. Kids love to feel included. My daughter calls herself my helper girl.

My second strength is competition. The book defines this strength as "you don't compete for the fun of competing. You compete to win." (Strengths Finder 2.0) I love a good race. The butterflies that I get in my stomach before a race is unlike anything I've ever felt. The excitement of choosing my race apparel, what song mix I want to listen to, and the thrill of talking to other runners before the competition begins lights my soul on fire. When that gun or blow horn or whatever it is they decide to sound goes off, it's like shock waves shoot through my entire body. Racing bring me to peace with myself. Racing gives me purpose and allows me to be a part of something that is bigger than myself. There is something so meaningful about being a part of a group of individuals all going toward the same goal. Maybe it's not running for you or even working out. Maybe it's being a part of a book club or a mommy group. Maybe it's a craft club or a volunteer organization. Whatever it is that lights your soul on fire, do it as a group. If there isn't a group in your town, make a group. Normally, competition has a negative connotation. But I say we change that. Competition helps us to become better versions of ourselves. Competition requires us to dig deeper than we ever have before. Competition makes us push and fight for more even when we think there is nothing left to give. It's why we don't have one insurance provider, one electric company, and one nail salon. We need competition to push ourselves to be better; just like in motherhood. Healthy competition is vital for growth.

My third strength is discipline. In the book, discipline is described as "the routines, the timelines, the structure, all these help create this feeling of control" (Strengths Finder 2.0). The more organized, the better. The cleaner the house, the less clutter on the counters, and a perfectly planned week makes my heart happy. Without these things, my world feels chaotic and stressful. I am not the mama who loves to get slime out on a raining day or spread play dough all over the floor. I don't enjoy crumbs on the floor and Oreo-covered faces. I am a firm believer that children need discipline and order. They need to feel protected and know that certain boundaries do exist even if they are going to test them one thousand times a day. Discipline is important in a society that is filled with instant gratification. You want a new hair product, order it; and boom, Amazon Prime will deliver it within two days. You're bored, here's an iPad with over two hundred games to keep you entertained. You want a new workout video, grab your iPhone and bring up thousands of workout videos in seconds. This predictability helps me make sense of the world around me even if my kids are driving me nuts. Kids love to test boundaries, so if this is your strength, teach them what boundaries exist.

My fourth strength is focus. I thrive in having a road map to a clear destination. In the book, discipline is described as "evaluating whether or not a particular action will help you move toward your goal" (Strengths Finder 2.0). I remember in middle school getting a gift from a good friend for my birthday; it was a lava lamp. So cool, right? Now, any other normal middle school girl would have been totally stoked with the hot lava colors bubbling to the top. But remember, I wasn't your normal middle schooler. I remember saying to my mom, "What am I going to do with this?"

She said, "It's to enjoy, Jenny. No, it won't help you do your homework or get an A on a school project. It's a gift. Be grateful."

When I am focused on a particular goal, that is all that exists in my world. It encompasses me whole. I wasn't one of those kids who barely opened a book and passed. I had to work my butt off to get As and Bs. The perfectionist in me demanded it. I hated organized exams. My nerves always seemed to get the best of me, and I was second-guessing every decision I made. I went to school with some extremely smart individuals. Some of my classmates scored in the 29s and 30s on their ACT but didn't make honor roll. I scored a 19 on my ACT. I was pretty sure there was a monkey who scored 22 and another person who chose C for every answer and got a 20, but that was beside the point. I graduated with high honors from my high school because nothing came between the focus I had to achieve the tasks at hand. I worked my butt off and became the first person in my family to graduate with a college degree. I became one of five individuals chosen to write my commencement speech for the graduating class. My ability to focus has led me to success time and time again. If this is your strength, use it to your advantage. If you're planning a birthday party, garage sale, baby shower, or anything in between, use your focus to crush your goals.

My last strength is futuristic. The book describes futuristic as "you are a dreamer who sees visions of what could be and who cherishes those visions" (Strengths Finder 2.0). When I was in college, my dream was to write speeches for the White House. I thought the best place for me to be was in the center of it all on Capitol Hill. My junior year, I went to Washington, DC, for the summer and worked for a fundraising organization on the Hill. It was cutthroat work. If you have never been to the Hill, it is filled with energetic young adults who are all trying to work their way to the top. The days are long, and the nights even longer. It was completely normal to leave on the train around 6:30 a.m. and not get home until 11:00 p.m. after a fundraising night. They say Vegas is the city that doesn't sleep, but I beg to differ. This is the part in a normal inspirational book where I tell you that I worked until I reached my dream. Don't take this the wrong way; I had a wonderful experience in the heart of DC that summer, but I just wasn't sold on moving there after graduation. I never would have known that if I hadn't taken that leap of faith my junior year. I am a planner and a forward thinker. I sometimes think so much about future plans and goals that I forget to enjoy the moment. I am so busy planning my child's next birthday party that I miss them laughing with each other about something silly. I used to love watching The West Wing during my college days. Jed Bartlet, the fictional democratic president, was an incredible character; and Aaron Sorkin, the writer and producer of the show, was pure genius. After any task was completed, Jed would say, "What's next?" He rarely rejoiced in victories and was always looking toward the future. The world is full of possibilities; some as big as a career change or a move across the county, and some are as small as teaching your child how to use the bathroom or tie their shoelaces. As long as we are always looking toward the future, the past cannot hold us back. That's what makes your journey in motherhood unique. You plan the road map for the kind of life you're going to live.

You can't be anything you want to be, but you can become a lot more of who you already are. Instead of wasting precious time correcting our weakness, we can go a lot further by focusing on our strengths. The time that is needed to correct our weaknesses is going to take so much more out of us than the energy needed to capitalize on our strengths. Say, for example, our weaknesses start at a negative twenty-five and our strengths start at a forty-five. We are going to be so much further along if we start at the forty-five instead of the negative twenty-five. Focus on being an expert at the things you do well and I promise you will flourish.

You are given these unique strengths for a reason. You aren't given these gifts to be locked up inside you and wasted because you are too scared to use them. Courage is doing the things that scare you. Courage is choosing to do it even when you aren't sure of the outcome. Courage is inside you.

I had the opportunity to speak at a women's health and wellness event in the basement of a Baptist Church. The tickets were sold out, and fifty-five women were scheduled to attend. The ages of the women ranged from twenty-five to seventy-five. This was my first public speaking gig, and I was tickled. Some people would rather die than speak in public; me on the other hand, this was my stage. This was my chance to share my stories with the world in the hopes that it would help other women share theirs.

From a very early age, I always loved speaking. I loved show-and-tell in grade school and presenting at the science fair in middle school. I loved when I got to share my book review with the class. I loved having an audience. My senior year of college, I had the privilege of speaking on behalf of the Illinois Map Grants for my university. I spent hours preparing that speech and rehearsing it in front of the mirror in my college dorm room. There were camera crews everywhere, the entire university was present, the board of directors and thousands of people were watching it live on their televisions at home. It was an incredible moment in time and one that I would always remember fondly. I remember the incredible honor it was to speak at my best friend's wedding. I enjoyed the preparation all the way down to the presentation.

Speaking is a gift. It is the ability to influence those around you through stories, lessons, and advice. Speaking is a sacred talent and if used correctly, can help change the world. The women's event I was speaking at was about self-love. I knew I wanted to get my audience tangible advice. I didn't want to simply tell them that they should love themselves; they already knew. What I wanted to do was give them simple tactical advice; things they could easily implement into their daily lives that helped them love themselves better. I can only describe the speech as a blackout. I got so in tune with my message that it was almost like an out-of-body experience. It was as if I was watching myself speak like I was a member of the audience. My speech started flowing, and my brain was locked in. I never once got tripped up or lost my train of thought. I was in the zone. Once the speech was over, I got back to my table of friends and asked what they thought. They looked at me with blank stares. "It was awesome," "You did amazing," and "Everyone loved it." I literally had no idea how the speech went until I watched it for myself. After watching the video, I was so stinking proud of myself. It really did go awesome. One friend asked me if I was so relieved it was over. To which I replied, "No, not at all. I want to do it again." Speaking gives me a high. When you love doing something, you don't want it to end. You want to continue riding that high. Find your high.

I was made to encourage and inspire women to be better versions of themselves. This was my vision of what I would want to hear from a speaker. It was my story. My life. My experiences. My legacy.

I used to think that the saying "You are one decision away from a completely different life" was so silly. I always thought there was no way I could change my life by simply changing one thing. Boy, was I wrong. Waking up one hour earlier than I normally do can change my life. Spending thirty minutes a day exercising can change my life. Writing half a page of my book four times a week can change my life. Starting a motivational Facebook page for women can change my life. Spending twenty minutes a day reading to my children can change my life. Scheduling a date night once a week with my husband can change my life. Helping others around me achieve their goals can change my life. Volunteering for an organization I feel passionate about can change my life. Writing in a journal can change my life. Starting a new hobby can change my life.

There are millions of small things you can do today that will change your life. They don't have to be massive changes like moving across the county, quitting your job, or never eating fast food ever again. How do you eat an elephant? One bite at a time. I didn't run a marathon, write seven thousand words for my book, start a Facebook page, send my subscribers inspiring e-mails, and speak at a women's event all in one day. I started to train for a marathon one day and kept building on that in the days that followed. I started to write a book when my son was three months old; he is now five years old. I started an inspirational Facebook page for women that started with two likes and now has over two hundred followers. All your dreams are not going to come true overnight. It is a marathon, not a sprint. Things take time to develop, and they aren't all going to happen on your timeline. A little progress here and a little progress there will compound over time and bring you closer to your overall goal.

Most of us are searching for something more—more meaning, more time, and more purpose. We feel as though something is missing. We can't create more time, but we can be wiser with the time we do have. Using our strengths to our advantage and finding meaning outside of our scheduled responsibility is vital to our overall health. Capitalize on your strengths and work to improve them with each passing day. I love to speak, but I am only going to get better at public speaking by speaking in public. I love to run, but I am only going to be able to run a marathon by training. I have always wanted to write a book, but I am only going to do it if I decide to start typing.

We all have strengths; even if we think we don't, we do. Don't say that you aren't good at anything. You're good at lots of things. You just need to narrow down your focus to a few things that you want to master. I'm not talking about a fancy degree, ten years of experience, and a degree to prove it. There are people who have less resources and less experience than you who are annihilating their goals. Don't get left behind because you simply cannot find the key to unlock your strengths.

CHAPTER 5

The Struggle Is Real

I did not come from a wealthy family. My mother and father divorced when I was seven years old. We lived with my grandmother until my mom could save enough money to purchase a home. At fifteen, I got my first job as a dishwasher at the local tearoom. I would make forty dollars for an afternoon, and I felt like an extra in the Notorious B. I. G. music video "Mo Money Mo Problems."

Once I was old enough to waitress, I started doing that as well. From as far back as I can remember, I would steal my mom's bills and send in payments. She reminded me time and time again that I didn't need to do that, but I didn't care. She was creating a better life for us, and I wanted to help her in any way that I could. She worked her butt off to provide a great life for me, and I will be forever grateful for her sacrifice. She would continually go without so that I wasn't left wanting for anything. I was fortunate enough to go to a private high school with the help of my close friends and extended family. When it was time to go to college, I applied tirelessly for every academic scholarship I could find. Between loans, grants and scholarships, I was able to attend Bradley University. I graduated with honors, belonged to numerous organizations, and had a wonderful all-around college experience.

My mother always viewed our financial situation as a burden. She was always wishing she could do more for me. She viewed herself as a failure because she divorced her husband. When in fact, it was quite the opposite. I became the person I am today because of my mom. I would never have worked hard, dug my boots in, and fought for what I wanted in life if I would have been given everything from the start. I have met people who are given everything, and it doesn't make them a better person. My background, childhood, and hard work have molded me into the person I am today. The struggle that some of us go through is real, but it will only make you stronger in the end. My upbringing, like many of you, has transformed something negative into something positive. I am thankful for how I was raised and being taught the meaning of hard work. My childhood taught me so much about working hard for what I wanted, not settling for mediocrity, and realizing that a modest life can bring immense joy.

Raising a family is complex and multifaceted, but don't think for a second that you're not a good mom because you can't afford a new car, name-brand clothes, or a spot on every select sports team. The lessons you are teaching your children about hard work, dedication, and commitment are so much more valuable than anything that new sports car can teach them. You may think that by giving your child everything you are being a good mother. By giving them everything and never having them work for anything, you are reinforcing the fact that hard work isn't necessary in life. The world doesn't need another generation of entitled children who think the world owes them something. The world needs diligent and compassionate adults to shape the future.

Now, onto the spousal struggle bus. I believe there is no single biggest earthshaking event that will happen to your marriage than that of bearing and raising children. It is a life-altering new beginning, and you can never go back to how it was before you became parents. For some reason, once this little miracle arrives in your arms, you begin to resent the one person who helped you bring this baby into the world. I remember having such a deep dislike for my husband after my first child was born, and I actually started to question these feelings. Like, seriously, "You didn't wash the dishes or take out the trash or empty the dishwasher or buy more diapers or wash the bottles or prep dinner or give me more time to relax." Ugh. I found myself absolutely resenting his very existence and wanting to shove his head in the toilet and flush it a few times. And then at the end of the night when he wanted to spend some time together and get closer under the sheets, ugh. No, thank you. I am lactating through my clothes, smell like a dirty diaper, and in a constant state of exhaustion.

I found myself holding grudges against my husband for all the things he wasn't doing instead of focusing on all the things that he did well. I failed to see how difficult the transition of becoming a father at age thirty-five was for him. It wasn't that my husband was giving me the bird, he was just trying to survive his new role of fatherhood. It took me years to finally understand this revelation. My husband does in fact love me deeply. He does, in fact, care about the children, and he is doing his very best. Just because his best doesn't look like my best, doesn't make his wrong. I will repeat. Just because his best doesn't look like my best, doesn't make his wrong. Your very best at motherhood probably won't look like his fatherhood, and that is okay. As women and men, we all have different strengths and talents. My husband is always great at making time to play hockey with our son or dress up Barbies with our daughter. He is amazing at finances, paying bills, grocery shopping, and planning family vacations. On the other hand, I prefer to meal plan for the week, take the kids to activities, and plan birthday parties. We are a team because we balance each other. It's not always fifty-fifty. In fact, it rarely is ever split evenly.

By holding a grudge against your spouse, the only person you are hurting is yourself. My dislike of him in the early years of raising children hurt everyone. In my head, I would add up all the things he was doing wrong, and as the list grew and grew, the angrier I became; until one day, I would lose my shit over the trash can being full. It wasn't that particular trash bag that was bothering me, it was all the other things that came before it. It was the straw that broke the camel's back. Instead of seeing any fault in myself for the way I was doing motherhood, I continually blamed him for everything I felt he was doing wrong. In the long run, did it really matter if the dishes were done that night? Nope, I was sure they would be there in the morning. Did the trash need to be taken out that instant? Nope, not unless it was spilling onto the floor that second. I had to finally take a hard look at myself and stop resenting his existence just because he didn't parent how I believed he should. How terrible would it be if we all parented the same way?

"Honey, I want to plan the birthday party."

"No, I want to do it."

"Sweets, can I pay for the school tuition?"

"No, I am doing it."

I think we would equally have the same problems in parenthood with grudges and resentment as we would with uniformity and sameness.

As a woman, we are told to give one hundred percent as a mother and one hundred percent as a wife. I'm not that great with math, but that equals two hundred percent, which is a completely unachievable goal. Talk about being set up for failure when it's not even humanly possible. There is no way you are ever going to be the best mother and the best wife at all times in your life. There are days where you are going to kill it as a wife and make the best meals and plan the perfect date nights and have the best conversations. Then, there are going to be weeks where you don't even make it to the grocery store, barely spend any time together, and are feeling pretty unconnected. Being a good wife means that your husband is, pardon my language, well fucked, well-fed, and well ironed. It is not our life's work as a wife to ensure that our husbands are well cared for at all times. If we cannot take care of ourselves and our personal well-being, then there is no way that we can take care of our husband's.

I'm not sure when being the busiest mom became such a sought-after title to win. Like, I woke up at 5:00 a.m. so I could do a yoga class; then fix a gluten-free, non-GMO breakfast, for my children; go to work all day; come home just in time to catch the PTO meeting where I needed to sell one hundred tickets for a fundraiser; then drive my daughter to dance and son to hockey practice; and then come home to make a three-course meal before bathing everyone, snuggling up for books, and then having a yoga session with the husband under the sheets before going to bed to do it all again tomorrow.

You are not my competition. I don't need to try to keep up with your schedule in order to validate my own. Your priorities and self-worth are not mine, and how you live your life is none of my business. There is no golden star for being the busiest mom of the week or the one who checked off three hundred and fifty things on her to-do list. Time spent on yourself and your family is never time wasted.

I hear moms talk about their schedules, listing off the fifteen things they are responsible for in the day and in the same breath complaining about how rundown and tired they are constantly. Hello! Didn't you just hear yourself say that you're overbooked? I understand that children need to be challenged in athletics, band, theater, arts, and any other extracurricular activity that sparks their interest, but they don't need to be in five. Pick one or two that they really love and stick with that for a while. Keeping your kids active is one thing, but sacrificing your sanity in exchange for ball practice three nights a week is just plain mad.

Instead of building each other up, we are tearing one another down with our thoughts and accusations. Like, "Oh, look, there is Andrew's mom who brought boxed sugar cookies to the school Christmas party again," or "Poor Chrysanthemum still isn't signed up for gymnastics yet. I guess her kids aren't a priority." Stop it. Instead, let's say, "That chick is rad for not caring about what other people think of her. I bet she is comfortable in who she is, and her kids are probably having a kick-ass childhood." Besides, who doesn't love those soft-baked, two pounds of icing, sprinkle-filled morsels anyway?

We applaud fathers for playing with their kids, driving them to practice, or taking them to the doctor. We may as well pin a gold medal on their shirt and have them go down in the world record book as the best dad that ever lived, period. As a mother, you are expected to do all these things plus another four thousand more. It is expected that you work your hands to the bone every day to provide the needs for your entire family; while in the same breath, fathers are applauded for walking their kids into school in the morning. When as a society did it become acceptable to hold mothers to these impossible standards? Last time I checked, it takes two to tango. Half male and half female. Parenting your children should be no different.

Moms are just as guilty of quiet judging. We see a father taking their kid to the dentist and smile as we walk by them thinking how nice it is for him to do that. Hold up. Wait a minute. Something ain't right. (Just like Sweet Brown's recollection of the fire in her apartment, "Oh Lord Jesus, there's a fire!") Why did we notice that? I am one hundred percent confident that if it were a mother walking her kids into the dentist, we wouldn't have blinked an eye. You want to know why. Because we have become so conditioned to the specific roles we play in parenthood—men work hard for the money and women are homemakers. Even if both parents work, the mother is still expected to take the children to the dentist. That's the social norm.

I'm calling BS. Moms need margarita nights and eating their weight in cheese dip. Moms deserve a lunch day with a gal pal or a quick weekend to some fun getaway or a manicure-pedicure date with an old high school friend.

We should not be living life trying to ensure we don't inconvenience our spouses. We shouldn't be timid or scared to ask for a break sometimes. We shouldn't feel like failures as a wife or a mom or a daughter or a friend just because we want some help. In fact, admitting you need help is one of the strongest things you can do. Everyone needs a break. Even you, supermama of the year, even you. By learning to recognize when your burning stick is almost at the end, this allows you to recalibrate, reload, and refocus your energy. Because a happy mom is the best kind of mom.

I never developed anxiety until I had children. I felt on the verge of a nervous breakdown most days. How am I supposed to work full time, do the laundry, grocery shop, cook, clean, go to appointments, get gas, run errands, drink enough water, exercise, call my mom, and spend time with my husband. It all was too much. I felt overwhelmed trying to attempt any of it. I worried about my children at school. I worried about them being under the watch of a grandparent or friend. I automatically went to the worst-case scenario. There was no gray area in my life; everything was either black or white. It was good or bad. There wasn't any room for neutral ground. I wasn't Switzerland. This was World War II.

Once my anxiety and depression got debilitating, I made an appointment with my doctor. I wrote down all my feelings, including but not limited to exhaustion, fatigue, stress, anxiety, depression, loneliness, nervousness and desperation. I finally decided that I needed to talk to someone. Someone who had probably witnessed these problems with hundreds of other people. My problems weren't new problems; they were just new to me. I kept asking over and over again, "Why does everyone else have it all together and I don't? What's wrong with me?" At the time, my doctor tried to explain to me how many people needed help at different times in their life to cope with their issues, and if I only knew how many other people didn't have it all together and blah, blah, blah. I wasn't hearing any of it because I was convinced that I was the one with the problem. He placed me on a low-dose anxiety medication, and for the first time in a long time, I slept through the night. I woke up with a newfound appreciation for good sleep. I felt better, my thoughts were positive, and I had a new outlook.

No one has it all together. I don't care how perfect their Instagram feed looks or how their Facebook stories are always color coordinated in the perfect shade of pink and white. I don't care that they appear to have the most perfect marriage and spend their time on social media platforms professing their love to one another. I don't care that they are continually going on expensive vacations, learning a new language, or backpacking through Europe. I don't care that they brag on their children about how they always get straight As, play two instruments, and already have six college acceptance letters by second grade. I don't care.

Trust me when I say that the perfect image they are trying to give off does not match the unfiltered version at home. No one has it all together, and if they tell you they do, just know that they are completely and utterly nuts, and you definitely don't need that kind of crazy in your life. So run.

You are human, not a robot. You don't run on mechanically programmed data throughout the day. You have feelings, wants, and needs. You are doing the best you can day in and day out. Some days will be better than others, and somedays will be the worst. But don't think for a second that their life is more glamorous than yours. Their life is filtered in a way that shows the good and hides the bad. I don't know about you, but I want to raise my kids in a world where perfect isn't something that is sought-after. I want them to know that growth is more important. Failure is acceptable because it means they are trying. I want them to know that they don't have to have it all together to start making progress. I want my children to show their true colors. You don't need to compare her perfect squares to your mom brain with twenty-seven tabs running at all times. You need to be a little bit better than you were yesterday.

Life is so noisy. There are times where I feel like I can't hear my own thoughts over the noise of the world. I am pulled in this direction because someone spilled their milk and another needs this snack opened. I am trying to talk to my husband over dinner about important things that are happening in our lives, and I cannot hear the words coming out of my mouth because the kids are laughing hysterically over something they find amusing. It's all so loud that I sometimes wonder how we focus long enough to get anything done. There's laundry, dinners, cleaning, lunches, homework, fundraisers, and snacks—thousands of thousands of snacks that need to be opened. It all becomes deafening at times.

I feel like I can never be present enough for one thing. Whether it's an important conversation with my spouse or a special moment with my daughter. My watch dings. I get an e-mail notification. Someone calls. A person wants to buy something I listed on Facebook Marketplace. Mindlessly scrolling social media accounts until you end up on your friend's sister's aunt's hairdressers page, and you aren't exactly sure how you got here in the first place.

Sometimes I wish the director of my movie will walk in and say cut just to stop the scene to give the actors a minute to use the restroom or freshen their makeup or take a break for lunch. But there are no breaks in life. It keeps going at an incredible speed. You can't slow it down, and you can't jump off. You're locked in for the ride.

The noise is beautiful, but so is the silence. Finding the time to talk about the hard things and the things that are on your heart is so important. We get dragged along this wild ride, and some of us never really coming up for air. We never really take it all in or truly enjoy the present.

Resistance is a bitch, isn't it? It's like there is this little "C U next Tuesday" in your head that is constantly trying to ruin your plans. She sucks any motivation that you might have to exercise. She even ate the last Girl Scout cookie and is a professional procrastinator. We all know what is good for us. We all know that it is necessary to have a source of income, pay bills on time, drink enough water, plan nutritious meals, raise our children to be kind people, and somehow find time for ourselves. We know what creates a somewhat balanced life and what brings us happiness. If you're anything like me, you also know what does not bring you happiness. For me, working out by running and weight lifting is a huge stress relief. I always feel so much better after I complete a good work out. I also know that failing to work out puts me in bad mood. Not drinking enough water gives me headaches and makes me tired. Failing to meal prep for the week creates stress at nighttime, and seeing my children act out for attention makes me sad. I know all these things, but for some reason, I still catch myself hitting that snooze button one too many times. I know that exercising in the morning sets my mood for the day. I am more productive, happier, and feel overall better when I make time for me in the morning. Then why do I let resistance control my actions? I know the behaviors that help me live my best life and those that threaten its very existence. Don't give that bitch her power. Don't second-guess it. Make your positive behaviors so repetitive that your brain doesn't even recognize that the behavior is a choice; it's an automatic action. The more positive actions you put together, the more repetitious your behaviors will become, and the less time your brain will have to talk you out of what needs to get done. Life is too short to hang out with bitches anyway, and resistance is definitely a bitch.

Isn't is incredible how small nuisances and inconveniences can turn into huge stress monsters? If you come to expect issues or problems in life, you will seldom be disappointed. It's when you expect your life to be absolutely perfect and things begin to go wrong that life gets really out of hand. People tend to become discouraged when expectations are left unmet. If you plan on having a good morning with the kids but your three-nager shows up in quite a mood in the morning, that is going to bother you. If you spill coffee on your new blouse or get stuck in traffic or the jack wad that always rides your bumper in the morning gives you the bird before your turn, it will be upsetting. When you don't get the promotion you expect to get, your sister-in-law is pregnant before you are, and it just seems like the universe is against you, breath. Nothing is as big of a problem as it seems.

I am not saying that you should expect bad things to happen to you. Not at all. Positive energy attracts positive things. What I am saying is that don't expect for everything to go your way all the time. If you are prepared for road blocks, detours, red lights, and railroad tracks, you won't be so angry when they happen. You are prepared for it already, and you know it is going to happen. You don't know when, but you know something will happen throughout the day that will throw you off-balance. Then, those small molehills won't seem like such gigantic mountains to scale because you already have your climbing shoes laced.

We don't need approval for anything. We are adults. We can drive to get ice cream, go to the gym, and decide to make dinner or go out with girlfriends. We are the captains of our own ships. The world does not get to decide who you are going to be and what you're going to accomplish. It does not give you a manual the minute you arrive to earth with all the information already filled out. It's completely blank. It's white space on tens of thousands of pages that are waiting to be written. You and only you allow what goes on those pages. Your past doesn't decide your future. Only you can decide.

There aren't any road maps in life, whether it's getting married, starting a new career, starting a new business, or raising kids. We all just figure it out as we go. We all have literally no idea what we are doing, and everyone is just holding on and doing their best. There isn't someone holding cones navigating where we should turn next. If you work in the country like me, the roads aren't even labeled with names; you just know whether to turn right or left at the stop sign. You decide whether you're going to take the right or left. I have been lost so many times I cannot count them on two hands and two feet. I get turned around and scared and start to panic. I'm lost. What if my cell phone dies or I lose reception? I only have one bottle of water and no food. Great, now I'm positive I'm going to die on a desolate country dirt road, and Dierks Bentley isn't coming my way singing "What Was I Thinking?"

CHAPTER 6

Appearance Is Relative

I'll never forget going to Savanah, Georgia, for my one of my good friends' bachelorette party. We stayed in a beautiful historic home that had a pool and all the amenities a group of girls ready to party could possibly need: fancy drinks, a photo booth, food, and bachelorette swag. The bride-to-be and I were getting ready for a fun night out. While changing into our dresses for the evening, she stopped what she was doing and said, "Oh my gosh, what happened to your boobs."

Being the good friends that we were, I laughed out loud and simply said one word, "Kids."

Coming from someone who had no kids, nor was that even in her realm of reality, she couldn't understand how they had changed so much from college. In her mind, whatever caused the gravity of the universe to shift and the shrinkage of breast tissue was not something that interested her. I don't blame her. It's not all glamorous, and until you actually go through the process, you have no clue what is about to head your way. In fact, if we know what we are getting ourselves into before becoming pregnant, the world population will most likely shrink in half. In order to save the conversation, my friend proceeded to tell me how flat my stomach still looked after birthing two children. Good save, girl. This conversation will forever be sketched in my memory.

Appearance is relative. My pre-pregnancy body will never look exactly the same. The number on the scale may be the same, but the person looking back at me has changed. My ab muscles are barely visible. There is loose skin in places that used to be as tight as a drum. My butt is flatter, and my boobs hang down farther than they ever have before. My kids question why my butt jiggles and why it's become as flat at a pancake. My arms sometimes wave back at me while I'm trying to wave at someone else. One nipple is permanently inverted and probably will be for the rest of my life. (Don't worry. My doctor has looked at this, and it isn't cancerous.) The number on the scale may match what it said prior to birthing children but my body itself will never match that again.

Maybe that's the point? Maybe going through something as powerful as bringing life into the world is supposed to change us. It's supposed to turn our world upside down, and once we experience it, we can never go back to who we are before. We have been through too much. We are forever changed. We have experienced almost the same pain as a man feels when he has the flu.

My metabolism has always been pretty fast, and it only took me a few months to get back to my pre-pregnancy weight after baby number one. It does not matter whether it takes you two months or five years or a lifetime to get back to a body you desire. Weight is relative. I may catch myself being envious of the mom next to me at pickup line because she has a rocking body. However, I bet it doesn't feel that way to her because her body has been through so much after children. Her body doesn't look like it did before kids either; no matter how fabulous it looks to the rest of the world.

We are only gathering information from that particular moment in time; a brief snippet of her life. We only see her in the present time. She remembers her past body as well as the present one. For all you know, you could be one of those moms to someone else. You could be the one who catches envious eyes from another mom because she admires you in some way. She wishes she has something that you have.

There are women out there who will give anything to have your stretch marks. They will give anything to have bags under their eyes and be covered in baby spit up. They long for a day where they can hold their own baby in their arms and wake up fifty times a night to make sure they are still breathing. Remember, there are people out there who will give anything to have your life. Let me repeat that. There are people out there who will give anything to have your life. Remember how lucky you are to have the burden of motherhood.

Weight is always relative. There is always going to be some mom with perkier boobs, a bubble butt, or gorgeous skin. There are always going to be moms with perfectly done hair and makeup for Saturday morning soccer practice and stiletto heels when they go out. If that is you, I applaud you. Those women amaze me how their ducks are always in a row. My ducks are always wandering off and getting distracted by something else. I barely look presentable for school drop-off in the morning, and I have forgotten mascara on one eye more times than I'd like to admit. I am the mother who realizes that her underwear is on inside out after it's far too late in the day to change them the right way. I am always running to beat the bell for school in the morning, and I give my children boxed french toast sticks for breakfast. My daughter's teacher knows that I am going to bring her brush and ponytail holder into school to fix her hair.

I am not a rock star, and I don't have it all together. Moms that like to wear sweatpants and drink wine on the weekends while the kids run around—those are my people. Moms who look like they just survived a magnitude 7.5 earthquake after bedtime—those are my girls. Moms who serve wine and beer at birthday parties are fabulous. Moms who wonder if it's too late in the day to drink coffee or too early for happy hour—they are my spirit animals.

I am 5'7" and one hundred and thirty six pounds. Did I just tell the entire universe what I weigh? Yep, sure did. When I got married in 2011, I was one hundred twenty pounds. I would like to think that most of that is muscle now, but who really knows. Our appearance is relative. What is perfection to one person won't be perfection to the next. What is a healthy weight to one, won't be healthy to the next.

Always remember that you are beautifully and wonderfully made. You are exactly where you are meant to be at this time. You are not defined by your physical appearance but rather the size of your heart. Don't let the media fool you into believing otherwise. Almost all those models are photoshopped anyway. No child wants a genetically modified mom. They want their mom.

The best thing you can do for your mom self is to stop comparing your current situation to anyone else's. You're comparing coffee to wine, and it will never be a fair playing field. Trust me, I have tried. You're comparing your beginning to their middle. Or their end to your beginning. For all you know, the president of the PTO could have been working tirelessly with a trainer for the last year to get in shape. Another mom with an awesome body teaches yoga three times a day to stay fit. Another mom has a membership to the local gym and does CrossFit three nights a week. Comparing yourself to them is only going to make you feel worse. Compare yourself to the person you were a year ago or the person you were last week. Whatever you do, don't compare yourself to the woman next to you. No woman ever has to give up her crown for the woman next to her to shine.

You start to realize that your self-worth isn't defined by the shirt you wear to Super Bowl Sunday. You aren't defined by how fresh your hair is or how often your eyelashes touch your eyelids. You aren't defined by the thickness of your brows or the color of your skin. You aren't defined by how manicured your nails are or the designer purse you carry. Your self-worth isn't wrapped up in lavish vacations or the car you drive to work.

You start to realize that self-worth isn't something that money can buy. You start to understand that self-worth is how you feel about you. It's not what your husband thinks about you or your mother-in-law or your friends. Self-worth is how you feel in the skin you're in. It's about how much you love yourself and the life you're living. Self-worth is less about the materialist things and more about enjoying the life you're living. The only opinion that really matters is your own.

There's always going to be moms who appear to have it more together than you, and there will always be the hot mess express moms too. You're most likely somewhere in the middle, and there's nothing wrong with sitting in the middle of the class.

CHAPTER 7

Let Kids Be Kids

Now, this chapter may be difficult for some moms to digest. This idea that we need to raise our children to be these perfect beings that get straight As, play multiple sports, be active in the band, perform in two plays a year, and have time for friends and family is absurd. How about we focus on making sure they are good people and not entitled assholes? How about raising them to be kind and inclusive to everyone? How about instilling things like hard work and dedication? Think of how better off the world will be if it were filled with nicer people instead of well-educated people. Instead of everyone stepping on each other's heads to get to the top, we help everyone cross the finish line together. The more one person wins the more we all win. The impact we can make on the world will be tenfold as opposed to a few people basking in their own glory. When I ran my marathon, I was surrounded by the most helpful, encouraging, and positive people I had ever been around. No one cared about how fast their time was even though this was a Boston qualifying race. Every runner wanted to help the runner next to them cross the finish line. It wasn't a matter of which runners would beat out their competition. It was about runners competing against themselves to beat their own best times. These are the kind of races I can get behind. No one is stepping on anyone else's toes to get to the top. Everyone is encouraging one another to reach their own personal best. Everyone has their own perception of success, and there isn't one model out there that matches the next one. That's the beauty of individuality.

When did the idea of success for children become so narrow-minded? They have to go to college, they have to have an internship, and they have to be in the top percentage of their class. Children have a right to grow up and be who they choose to be, not who their mom or dad wants them to be. They have the God-given right to choose, and it isn't your right to revoke that choice because of your own wishes and dreams. Just because you never won a state title in football when you were in high school doesn't mean that your son wants that title. Just because you wanted to qualify for the state track meet does not mean that's what your daughter has pictured for her sports career. Just because you were a legacy at a sorority for XYZ Fraternity doesn't mean that he or she wants to follow in your exact footsteps. Stop living vicariously through your children. It's not their dream. It's your dream, and since your dream of high school sports, music, theater, band, etc. is over, it's over. It's their turn to decide where there future takes them, and it is your job to get out of the way. Yes, of course it's your job to raise them and guide them along the way, but don't hinder them because you have this preconceived image of what you want their future to look like. It's not fair to your kids.

If I am being completely honest with you, which is scary for me because anyone can read this book, my mother was not exactly happy with all my decisions. I know this is very hard to believe considering I am an only child and my mother stopped at perfection, but it's true. My husband is nine years older than me, and we met in a very non-traditional setting. The highs were high, and the lows were the lowest of the low. We went through more in the first several years of dating than some couples experience in their entire relationship. I knew it wouldn't be easy, and I think he knew the same about me, but we believed it would be worth it. If we could get through the hard stuff in the beginning, we could get through anything. But my mom didn't want that. She envisioned me going off to college and meeting a doctor or a lawyer and never having to worry about anything. She didn't want me to have the same life she did. She didn't want me to have a long-distance relationship or miss out on anything that college had to offer. But those were her dreams, not mine.

The pressure we put on our kids isn't healthy. It's selfish and not helping them grow into the people they are meant to become. There is a belief that in order to make the right decisions for our children, those decisions must be made by us. In actuality, they are most like creating resentment from their children for not allowing them to choose the life they want to live. I hate to break it to you, but fewer than 2 percent of NCAA athletes will go on to play professional sports. Less than 2 percent. The odds that your son will play for the Cleveland Cavaliers is so extremely slim.

As I sat at my son's soccer game, I overheard two parents complaining about their son's lack of interest in the soccer game. Every time he would come over for a water break, they would tell him, "You better kick the ball this time," "Pick it up," "When are you going to score a goal?" The small child was devastated, and the more they got on him, the worse it got. They even said things to the crowd like "This child is going to drive me to drink" and "He isn't going to the birthday party today." I sat there feeling so extremely sad for this small child. This was probably the first time he engaged in organized sports, and what were his parents teaching him? "You have to be better. You aren't good enough. We are taking things away from you." This child was four years old. Four years old. This was supposed to be a fun introduction to soccer for children who had never played on a team before. These parents were not only embarrassing themselves but their child as well. This was my first introduction to the world of organized sports. Life isn't supposed to be neat and tidy; it's supposed to be lived. Teaching children that they must be perfect at all times to excel in life is setting them up for a life of disappointment and destitute.

Let's get back to the basics. Let's stop worrying and stressing about whether Johnny is going to be the rock star soccer player that his parents so desperately want, and let's start focusing on what's going to make him a successful adult. I fully understand that school is in place to educate and guide children through their early years of life. It is there so that they can learn to take instruction, grow their minds, and connect with the world around them. However, when did parallelograms or the Pythagorean theorem become more important than learning how to cook, change a tire, balance your checkbook, or file your taxes? I can recite all the states and capitals to this day, but if you ask me to drive a stick shift, every passenger in the car will have whiplash by the end. I know all about the war of 1812 and the presidents of the United States, but I can't change my oil to save my life.

We need to shift our focus of what is considered success and start preparing kids for the real world. My biggest problem with the college system is that they build you up to think that employers are literally waiting for you to graduate so they can give you an $80,000 job right after college. They make you believe that you can be anything you want to be if you put the work in. This is a false message of hope. You can become a lot more of who you already are, but you cannot be anything you want to be. The day I graduated from college, I thought employers would be fighting to hire me. Much to my dismay, this was so far from the truth. It was a time of recession when I graduated. Companies were cutting back on their workforce and shipping jobs overseas. The world had not seen a setback like this since the Great Depression. Investors lost hundreds of thousands of dollars, and companies were not looking to hire new college graduates. I was stunned. I mean, hello, I had arrived. I was young, full of ideas, highly motivated, and ready to be president of your company by the end of the first fiscal year.

In high school and college, the world is divided up into semesters. Each semester lasted a few months. But in the real world, time seems to move at a sloth's speed. Everything seems to take years to accomplish, and most days feel like Groundhog Day. There are hours spent at work, laundry when you get home, and dinner to cook, bills to pay, and kids to entertain. There is so many different things that are competing for your attention and not enough hours in the day to accomplish it all.

There are days where I feel like I am killing it in the mom category but falling short as a wife. Then other days, I am a rock star employee but a distant friend. I have learned to accept that I cannot give one hundred percent to each of the hats I wear all the time. Sometimes certain roles will be more important and get more of my time, and that's all right. I am human, not superwoman, even though my kids think I am. If we are going to let kids be kids, let's let moms be moms. There isn't one right way to be a mother just like there isn't one right way to be a child.

When we continually preach to our kids to be nice to others, not to bully, and to be a bucket filler, we also need to model that behavior. When we find ourselves excluding other people, judging them, and engaging in negative thoughts, we need to recognize that and redirect our energy into something positive. I think we have become so quick to point out the flaws of our children that we fail to realize our own shortfalls. When I am having a bad day, I allow it and my husband allows it. We both understand that it is a rough day and tomorrow is a new chance for a fresh start. However, children are not allowed to have bad days. Things that upset a child seem so trivial to us because we have much bigger fish to fry. Do you remember when you were getting ready for your first prom? Your hair had to be just right, you searched tirelessly for the perfect dress, and your nails and toes had to be freshly painted. Your flowers had to be the right color, and everything had to be absolutely picture-perfect. And if it was anything less, think tears, tantrums, and the world coming to an end. Looking back, it's pretty clear to see that prom wasn't as nearly a big deal in the grand scheme of life as we made it out to be at the time. Try telling a high school junior girl that prom isn't a big deal. It's all relative. To that seventeen-year-old, prom is the most important thing in her life up to this point. We were once those little kids, too.

CHAPTER 8

We Make Time for What's Important

After becoming a mother, I had to become much more intentional with my time. When I used to hear people talk about being intentional with their time, I never really understand what they meant. Aren't we all intentional with our time? We decide to do something and do it. Isn't that making the decision to do it? Not exactly. There's much more to it.

In the age of technology, we have so many things that are competing for our attention. We have endless e-mails to respond to, apps to check, permission slips to fill out, activities to attend, meetings to make, water to drink, sleep to be had, baths to complete, laundry to fold, dishes to wash, and the list goes on. If I do not intentionally plan out my day and make time for the things I want to get to, it won't happen. As I sit here and write these words, the playroom directly across from the kitchen is a complete disaster. Like, magnetic tiles all over, naked babies, Legos, dinosaurs, books, play food, puzzles, and everything in between. The type A personality in me is begging me to go over there and organize it all just to have it all torn apart when the kids get back from grandma's. I have to force those thoughts out of my head because it won't help me achieve my goals for the day. In the grand scheme of things, does it matter if the playroom is cleaned?

Will I love for it to be clean? Of course. Is it going to ruin my day if it isn't cleaned? Absolutely not. There's only so much time that I have to get the things done that are on my heart, and if I don't specifically map out how I am going to get it done, I'll fall short. I have goals that I want to crush, dreams that I want to check off my list, lives to change, and people to motivate. That is the stuff that lights my soul on fire, not cleaning the playroom.

I started a motivational, inspirational Facebook page for women to remind them that there is an entire village of women who are rooting for their success. I never really ever thought about doing something like that. What if people think it's silly? What if I get made fun of? What if they don't like it? I am a thirty-one-year-old wife, mother of two, full-time employee, head chef, cleaning lady, laundry doer, and everything in between; and I am scared of what an internet troll might think of my Facebook page. How absurd does that sound when you put it that way?

A girlfriend sent me a text message this past week and said, "You motivated me. I ran three miles instead of two today. Thanks!" It was such a simple compliment, but it touched my heart in ways I could not explain. I inspired someone. I helped someone achieve their goals. I made a difference in someone's life. It hit me right then and there that if I could change her life, how many other lives could I change? I decided to create a community of women who all root for each other, inspire one another, and speak encouraging words despite their differences. There is so much we can learn from one other if we just take the time to listen.

It's not that you don't have time for your dream; you are lacking the necessary motivation for your dream. When you're excited about something and it makes your heart explode with happiness, you will always find the time. If it's not that important to you, you will find an excuse. I planned a surprise party for my mom's sixtieth birthday party, and when her friends asked me what was new in my life, I preceded to tell them that my kids were both in preschool and busy with soccer and gymnastics. I was training for a half marathon, coaching grade school track and working on writing a book. They all looked at me with blank stares and said, "How do you have time for all that?"

I looked back at them with equally blank stares. "You make time for what's important." I get up early, carve out time, rely on my husband and grandparents to pick up the slack, and become intentional with my time. I say no to going out to eat or lavish vacations if they don't fit into my plan. My entire life is not going to be made up of sluggishly getting out of bed each day waiting for the time to pass before I can crawl in it again. Life is meant to be lived and I want my children to work hard for the goals they want to achieve. Just because you become a mother does not mean that your entire life stops dead in your tracks. Just because you want the very best for your children doesn't mean that you sacrifice your own best self. Loving someone else does not require you to loss yourself in the process. Just because you're a wife and mother doesn't mean that you can't have your own dreams and aspirations that have nothing to do with your family.

I hear these excuses all the time. "I don't have time to pursue my dreams" or "I don't have any hobbies or interests" or "I'm boring, and there isn't anything that I could do" or "It's already been done." I hear these excuses all the time, and that's exactly what they are excuses. Excuses that prevent you from taking action towards your goals. Of course it's already been done. Everything in this world has been done. That's why there are more than one photographer, writer, climber, runner, dancer, doctor, dentist, lawyer, teacher, preacher, mother, and father. You do things differently than anyone else. You are unique. There is no one else in the world exactly like you. There is no one else out there who has the exact same story as you do. The things you have experienced in your life, the ups, the downs, the hardships, and the triumphs are unlike anyone else. You have a unique story that is waiting to be told.

You don't have to have a degree from a university or be an expert in your field to share your story. You have to be authentic. You have to be real. You have to believe that what you can offer the world is unique. You have to believe that one person can change the world. You have to have confidence in yourself and your ability to make it happen. You have to have everyday courage.

We live in an age where anyone's voice can be heard. There are social media outlets, blogs, podcasts, videos, books, tutorials, and so much more where you can make your voice heard. There are thousands of people who are further along in their journey than you are simply because they decided to take a step forward. I recently looked at my screen time on my phone and found that I spend twenty-three hours a week on my phone. Twenty-three hours. That equates to three and a half hours a day of screen time. Of the twenty-three hours, ten and a half were spent on social networking, four and half were spent on productivity, and almost two hours were spent on creativity. That's almost one full day spent on my cell phone doing something. I encourage you to check where you are spending your time. It's really eye-opening to see where our time is spent. That's almost twenty-four hours that I could be spending working on my goals. Maybe your screen time is more or less than mine, but don't sit here and tell me you don't have time to work on your own goals. Your problem is you haven't made your goals a priority. You choose to let other things win. The laundry, the kids, the binging of shows, the ladies' nights, or the couch time. You have literally sketched into your brain that your schedule is full. The second a new idea enters into your brain—well, what if—your brain is already squashing it, saying, "Nope, we are already full over here." And with a mindset like that, you probably won't try anything new.

I'm sure I am the odd one out here, but I don't watch TV. I never sit down and turn on a show or binge on Netflix or get hooked on a new TV show. One reason is I don't know how to work our television that comes with four remotes. Second, I literally don't have time. The second I sit down, my mind races to everything I can be doing instead of sitting on the couch. I don't look down on people who watch television. I simply choose not to engage in this leisure activity.

It's okay for you to work your day job and spend your nights and weekends working on your dreams. No one said that we can only have a few titles that only include corporate employee, mother, and wife. Just like Daniel Tiger's Neighborhood, "You can be more than one thing." If it's on your heart, it's there for a reason. It's not going anywhere, and the more you ignore it, the larger the chance becomes of you not fulfilling it. It's okay to get up early and work on your goals. It's okay to spend time on something you want to late at night. It's acceptable to not spend all your time showing up for everyone else. I am a happier mother, wife, friend, and daughter when I spend time doing something I enjoy. When all I do is give and give until there is nothing left, I feel terrible. I feel worn down, unhappy, and frustrated. When I take time to go for a run, paint my nails, do a face mask, write my book, or create a video, my mood is improved. I don't feel like I am burning the stick at both ends. I don't feel like I am treading water just trying to keep my head above the waves. I don't feel like I am screaming for help and no one hears me. I feel fulfilled, content, and happy. And a happy person is the best kind of person.

We have a commitment to ourselves, our children, and our spouses, to reach our full potential. Start treating yourself the way you do your family, your friends, and your coworkers. You won't cancel plans with them or push aside their dreams because they are too big. Hell no! You will be right there with them, cheering them on along the way. Start being your own cheerleader. If you don't cheer for yourself, why should anyone else?

Hope is not a plan. Hoping the stock market goes up is not a plan. Hoping your spouse will help you reach your goal is not a plan. Hoping that dinner will somehow appear on the table and the dishes will get cleaned and is not a plan. It takes planning, preparation, and scheduling to make it all work. I once read a quote that says, "If you fail to plan, you plan to fail." If you fail to plan healthy meals for the week, you will likely make unhealthy choices out of desperation. If you fail to plan a date night once a week, you'll be sitting with kids seven nights a week. If you fail to carve out time to exercise, meet a friend for dinner, or volunteer at school, it will likely not take place. In order to be successful in a world that is constantly pulling us in different directions, we must be disciplined.

Do we ever put ourselves as a priority? I mean, really. Do we ever make a list of things that need our attention and make sure we pencil in time for ourselves? Do we ever make intentional time to work toward something that's a passion or goal for us? We are intentional about our grocery list, laundry, soccer practice, baseball clinics, and family trips. Some of us are even as intentional about date nights once a week and where we plan on spending family holidays. We are intentional about hiring tutors for our kids and enrolling them in elite sport leagues and organizations. We are intentional about ironing our spouse's shirts and ensuring they have a hot meal and an active sex life. Where in that equation do we make time for ourselves?

We will never disappoint our children or cancel our plans with our husband, but we continually put ourselves last. It's not about you coming first among your children and spouse, it's about saying, "Me too." I am a priority. This is my life. Just like the Imagine Dragons song, when my days come to an end, I want to say, "I did it all."

CHAPTER 9

Measuring Your Success

Your success will depend on how long you can endure sucking until you perfect your art. Chrissy Teigen didn't become an exceptional cook by never cooking because she was worried it would taste awful. Jenna Kutcher didn't just wake up one day and say, "I'm going to empower women and develop a kick-ass podcast overnight." It took work. Hard, grueling work. Becky Thompson of Scissortail SILK didn't start as a bestselling Christian author and podcast guru. She began her life as a lifestyle wardrobe blogger. Rachel Hollis didn't start her multimillion-dollar media company overnight. She worked for six years on it before even taking a paycheck. Joanna Gain's first home renovation looked drastically different than her final fixer-upper. The point is all these empowered, beautiful women had to start somewhere. They have grown leaps and bounds since they first began their journeys to success. Your journey has to start somewhere. Making small steps toward your goal will compound over time. You just have to keep your eye on the prize.

Successful people have things in common. They tend to get up early. Do you know the most successful people in the world get up two hours before they have to be at work? Our brains are sharpest in the morning, and successful people know they can't waste their precious brainpower sleeping. Successful people take care of their bodies by working out, eating right, and exercising their mind. They don't drink, smoke, or binge excessively. They are responsible with their finances. They work hard.

Unsuccessful people also have things in common. They make excuses for why they aren't successful. They blame their family, friends, and the universe for why things don't go their way. They surround themselves with other pessimist people just like themselves. They wallow in their self-misery. They tend to do everything in excess. They stay up late and rarely take care of their bodies or spend their money wisely. There is no order in what they do. They make excuses.

You get to decide every single day if you are going to be a success or a failure. We will never say, "Look at Jessica. She is so successful because she makes up excuses all the time" or "Look how successful Dave Ramsey is because he is so careless with his money." Those things don't go together because the adjective to describe the person doesn't match the individual.

I'm not stating that all successful or unsuccessful people do everything on this list. Sure, there are successful people who drink excessively or don't have their finances in order, but for the most part, successful people have similar routines, characteristics, and values as other successful people. Successful people surround themselves with other successful people.

Should winning in the present take precedence over growing in the future? In other words, should the immediate need to win and see results instantly outweigh the bigger difference that can come from dedicated hard work and perseverance? We live in a time of instant gratification. We expect to order an item online and have it delivered to our door the next day. We presume to move up at work quickly and without interference. We anticipate we will meet our partner, fall in love, and have kids by a certain age. Everything is quick, and if it isn't quick, we immediately become discouraged, distressed, and disheartened. We give up too quickly on our dreams for fear we aren't making adequate progress in the direction of our goal. The root of the problem is where we come up with this timeline in the first place. Who are we to say that goal A has to be met by a certain time, and if it isn't, we give up on the goal all together. The time is going to pass anyway no matter how much you want it to slow down. If you give up on a goal just because it's going to take awhile to get there, you need to reevaluate your thought process. If it were easy, everyone would do it. But since it's not easy, it's going to take work.

I think too many of us in our adult lives think that once we've made it, that's it. Once we land the job, the guy, and the kids, there isn't anything else. Too often we feel that we should be content with what we have and not want for anything more. Once we stop trying new things, we fail to grow. Once we get too content in our daily lives, we never step outside the box for something new. Mediocrity becomes the norm. It's always better to keep growing than stay perfect in mediocrity. The lessons you learn from trying something and failing will always outweigh never trying in the first place.

There is tremendous growth that can take place in any stage of life if you're willing to go for it. You want to start a hobby class where you paint with your girlfriends, do it. You want to write a book, do it. You want to start a blog, create a template. You want to join a workout class, sign up. You want to learn calligraphy, a new instrument, or take up paining, the time is now.

Even writing this book, there are days or moments where I'm unsure if I'm on the right path, if I have bit off more than I can chew, or worse, if I will even complete it. There are times where I am anxious about how it will be received. When the negative self-talk enters my head, I have to push it aside. I have to train my brain to stay on the course, keep my eye on the prize, and put one foot in front of the other. Every day isn't going to be a five-thousand-word-count day. You're not going to kill it every single day at work or be mom of the year three hundred sixty five days a year. You're not going to be the best wife every second of every day. That's perfectly okay. As long as you are doing a little bit every day to reach your goal, you're on the right path. A bunch of small building blocks put together over time creates a much larger and unbreakable wall. Without the small blocks, the wall won't be able to stand. It's the pieces that are laid meticulously in the beginning that give it the most solid foundation.

I didn't always want to write a book. I wasn't one of those children who drew pictures and scribbled notes and daydreamed about being an author. I created something new out of a void I believe existed. I wanted a community to feel connected to. I wanted support and a listening ear. I wanted a tribe of women to make me feel like I wasn't messing up my kid from the start. I saw a void, and I wanted to fill that void with my experiences.

My book journey began when my son was about two months old. I felt a desire in my heart and a real need for women to start telling the truth behind motherhood. Sure, ladies, having a child was one of the most amazing and incredible things I had ever accomplished. However, no one talked about the raw, untouched details. No one told you that you literally could not shave your lady parts and you were constantly wondering why your underwear was wet. No one told you that you would be scared to shit after childbirth because you were worried that your insides would fall in the toilet. No one talked about postpartum hair loss, battered nipples, and sleepless nights. Some of my darkest days took place after my son was born. I had major postpartum depression, but at the time, I couldn't recognize it for what it was—a completely debilitating disorder. I convinced myself that everyone else had this thing called motherhood figured out. I was the one with the problem. I kept it to myself and tried to deal with it the best way I knew how—through exercise, self-care, and relying on my family and friends for support. It's always so much clearer looking back. Today, I can identify exactly what was going on and what needed to take place in order to feel better. Man, what I would have given to have one mama tell me it was going to be okay. One mama to hug me on the playground and invite me over for coffee or wine. One mama to see the desperation in my eyes and the unsure voice in my chest. Just one mama to tell me that she, too, had been there, and it was going to get better, so much better than I could ever imagine.

If only one mama reads this book and identifies with anything in here, let it be this. You are not alone. It's okay to be afraid. None of us know what we are doing. It's okay to cry and laugh all in the same hour. It's okay that your clothes don't fit and you forget your kid's backpack. It's all going to be okay. You know how I know this? I am living proof that colic babies, life-changing careers, and nights that never seem to end actually do. I came out on the other side, and I am better for having walked through that season of hardship. And you know what? So are you. You are stronger than you think and more driven than you know. The knowledge and experience you will gain during these times in your life will transform you into the person you are today. Without waking through those sleepless nights, and stepping on Lego pieces, will you ever truly appreciate the good times? The ones where you laugh until your stomach aches, snuggle until the sun comes up, and realize what it is like to have your heart walking around outside your body. These are the best days.

I want all mamas to know that it's all right to talk about the time you lost your shit because your daughter wouldn't stop arguing about which bow she wanted to wear. Or the time you let your kid poop outside because you knew he couldn't make it to the bathroom in time. Or that time you locked yourself in the bathroom and told the kids you were sick so you could take a shower in peace and quiet. That doesn't make you a bad mama. It makes you self-aware. You know when you need a break. You know when you need to recharge. You know when you need to pull back a little in order to be the best mama you can be for your babies. If you don't take care of yourself, how are you ever going to survive the day with those needy little people and be the snack slave they desire?

So how do you measure your success? Is your success measured by how many PTO meetings you attend and field trips you chaperon? Or how many times you make dinner each week and take kids to practice? Is your success defined by how your child does in the spelling bee or how many times your spouse has bought you flowers? Measuring your success isn't something that takes place outside of us; it's already there. (Just like Poppy from Trolls says, "Happiness isn't something you put inside you. It's already there.") There are several times in my life that something earth-shattering took place and forever changed the person I am. I can't go back to that other gal I was before because she isn't there anymore. She no longer exists. It might as well have been an entirely different lifetime ago. That's how far away she feels. The current gal, the one who is currently writing this book, has been through too much, experienced too many things, and is now on the other side to talk about it. She can't just snap her fingers and go back to the other woman. The wisdom, strength, knowledge, and power that she has exemplified cannot be taken away. She birthed two beautiful babies, spent twenty-one hours in labor without any medical intervention whatsoever, and nursed both children from her own body. She trained for six months to run 26 miles and did a celebratory jump afterwards to prove her strength. Those experiences forever changed the person. She'll never be who she was before. I think that's the point, right? We go through things in our lives that shake our souls alive. It changes us to our core. You should be proud of how far you've come and what you have accomplished regardless of what anyone else has to say about it. They don't define your success. Only you can define you.

CHAPTER 10

You Are More

I don't believe I am placed on this earth to go to my day job, parent, and then do it all over again the next day. Don't mistake that; I do enjoy the predictable routine that comes from work and motherhood, but I need something more. I yearn for something more. Something that will light a fire under my bottom and a desire in my heart. I need to challenge my mind and my ability. I want to step outside my comfort zone and do something new. I don't think I am destined to be ordinary. I think I am meant to be extraordinary. And guess what, so are you.

You are more than a mother. You are more than an employee. You are more than a wife. You have unique gifts to offer the world that don't involve washing bottles, bathing babies, and folding laundry. You are more than the PTO meetings you attend, the lunches you pack, and the sheets you change. There is more to your life story than making sure dinner is on the table by 6:00 p.m., your son's science project is going to get first place, and the valentines robots that you bring to school are just right. Damn, Pinterest made that one look so easy. You are more than the PowerPoint projects you create and the problems you solve from 9:00 a.m. to 5:00 p.m. You are more than the papers you grade, the patients you see, and the clients you please.

Stop gauging your self-worth on things that don't matter. I'm not saying that dinner isn't important or that you should hope your son gets fifteenth place at the science fair instead of first, but is it really imperative that dinner is done by six or that your son gets first place? I bet he will remember much more from the fair where he placed toward the end than all the ones he won first. It builds character. It builds an understanding of the world around us. It teaches our children that they won't be perfect in everything they do. Thank goodness. Because the world will throw them a bunch of curveballs, and if they crumble every time something doesn't go their way, what a hard life they will lead. Trust me, they will be better equipped for life if you don't try to catch them every time they trip. Teaching kids they must be perfect at all times to bring joy to their parents will set them up for disaster. The world doesn't need more entitled children, and you don't need one living under your roof either. Let's start basing our self-worth on doing what we enjoy, finding things that light our soul on fire, and living the very best version of ourselves. You don't need to have the perfect presentation or out of this world PowerPoints every time you get in front of your clients. You don't need to be the perfectly put together wife with full makeup, hair done, and a cute outfit every time your husband walks in the door while you patiently wait to take his briefcase.

You don't need me, your mom, your aunt, your crazy best friend, your spouse, or your boss to help you become who you are meant to be. With every fiber of my being, I believe that you have had the tools you need inside you this whole time. You just need the confidence to let it shine. Even though you're going to get dirty again, that does not prevent you from showering. It's a daily journey, just like self-improvement. So why do we stop improving ourselves because the journey gets tough? It isn't supposed to be easy. If it were easy, will there be any real satisfaction in doing it at all?

I am going to be completely honest. There is something about baring your soul to the world that is somewhat nerve wracking. Will I get a ton of negative reviews online about why I ever thought I am qualified to write a book? Will they laugh and make fun of my writing style? Will they completely tear me down one jab at a time? Probably. And that's okay with me because who are they anyway. Who are they to say who I can or cannot be? Who are they to tell me that I cannot accomplish my dreams? Who cares about them? Honestly, who cares?

I already have my cheerleaders. I have a mom who cheered for me when I shot at the wrong basket in a seventh-grade basketball game. I have my husband who entertains my crazy ideas even though he's afraid I'm borderline insane. I have two kindhearted, beautiful babies who tell me I'm the best mom ever even when I feel like I am failing at it all. I have a village of friends who are hilarious, supportive, and keep me grounded when the world gets crazy. I don't need your permission to go after my goals. I don't need your approval to reach for my dreams. I don't need your negative comments to make me question myself and feel bad about who I am. And guess what. Neither do you.

You don't need anyone's approval to live your life the way you want to. You don't need anyone's consent to try something new or want something more for your life. You don't need to take a poll of every human on earth to get a consensus on whether or not you should do whatever it is that you're questioning. Just start doing it. I literally peed down my leg while running on the treadmill today while yelling at my kids so they could hear me over the noise of the workout machine. I peed down my leg, stopped the treadmill, went to the bathroom, and then got back to it. If I can handle writing about being thirty-one years old and peeing myself then you can surely achieve whatever goal it is that you're working towards. There are hundreds of thousands of people who are doing more things than you are—not because they are more qualified than you but because they did it. They jump off that bridge headfirst and dive right in. You're on the sideline waiting for the perfect time to get in the game. You're hesitant that maybe it's not the right time or you don't have enough money to start your goal or your toolbox is missing the necessary wrenches to begin.

You don't have to have it all figured out to begin. You have to have a destination of where you want to go and a road map of how you're going to get there. Every turn doesn't have to be mapped out; you just need to know where to start and where you want to end up. Sometimes we make things too difficult. We overthink them to a point where we literally talk ourselves out of pursuing our goals because we think they will be impossible to achieve.

Everyone was once a beginner. Eminem, also known as Marshall Mathers, who is one of the greatest rappers of our time, was chewed up, spit out, and booed off stage. It took Thomas Edison one thousand tries to develop the light bulb. He had to fail that many times before he got it right. Marc Randolph, the co-founder of Netflix, was told time and time again, "That will never work." The birth of all great things came first with resistance. Anyone who had ever tried something new had to first believe that it could exist. Steve Wozniak, the inventor of the first home computer had to believe that this could exist and not only exist but change the world forever.

I didn't know how to parent a child before I became a parent. I didn't know what the steps were to writing a book before I researched it. I didn't know about risk management in agriculture before I began my career. I didn't know how to train for a marathon until I educated myself. If you never start, there is a one hundred percent chance you will never reach your goal. Your competition isn't other people. Your competition is yourself. Your competition is your negative self-talk, your procrastination, and your excuses. Compete against that. Make it a habit to work on your goals a little bit each week, and that will compound over time. Don't get discouraged that your dream is taking too long. The time will pass regardless.

I'm a dreamer. I find it fascinating that incredible ideas exist in the world and projects are being worked on that can change lives and people everywhere. So many people believe that so many things cannot be done before someone proves them wrong. There were many people who believed that home computers would never take off or you would never be able to carry a phone around with you all the time or that we couldn't go to Mars or have sliced bread or timed windshield wipers or electricity or just about anything else. All these things were impossible before they were proved possible. I love the story about the ordinary man who reached the gates of heaven and said, "Who is the best navy pilot of all time?"

And God responded, "Well, you, of course."

The man said, "I wasn't a navy pilot."

God responded, "You would have been the best navy pilot in history if you would have tried."

Our fear of trying has to become greater than our fear of not trying. We continually hold ourselves back from reaching our dreams because we are too afraid to fail. The best actors, singers, songwriters, authors, and artists would have never made it to where they are today if they would have been scared to fail. Most of them failed over and over and over again until they got their big break.

Throughout my life, I have learned more from the failures than I ever learned from all the success. I can have one hundred successes and one failure, but that one failure is forever sketched into my memory. The greatest leaders, inventors, entrepreneurs, and authors all experienced failure before success. The difference between them and you is that they didn't let that stop them. They get back up, brush off their knees, and get back to it. No great thing is ever achieved without diligence, failure, and hard work. You may think, I could never write a book. Well, I am living proof that you're wrong. You can write a book, and it can change lives if you only take the time to sit down and write it. Or maybe you don't want to write a book; you want to lose weight. You may think, I could never lose weight. There are people who have lost three hundred, four hundred, or five hundred pounds. You can do it; you're just unwilling to put in the time necessary to achieve the goal. You may think, I could never run a half marathon. Are you willing to create a running schedule, stick to it, drink enough water, and get enough sleep? If not, then you aren't willing.

Start talking to yourself like you do your family, your friends, and your children. You continually build them up to go after their goals, achieve more, and reach for the stars, but when it comes to yourself, "Naw, I couldn't do those things." You have to stop the negative self-talk. You are capable of so much more than you will ever realize. We make excuses because that's more comfortable for us than going after our dreams. The fear of someone making fun of us or falling flat on our face prevents us from reaching our full potential. I still have dreams about the time I walked out of the bathroom at the mall and had toilet paper attached to my foot and everyone laughed.

I was fairly young, yet I still remember how I felt being embarrassed and humiliated in a public setting.

You are never too old to set another goal or to dream a new dream. Imagine how incredible the world will be if every person focused on reaching their full potential. If we aren't so dang scared of failing; think of the possibilities that can be transformed into reality. We think failing is the worst thing that can ever happen to us. Talk to someone who has had to bury their child. Talk to someone who has lost a loved one to cancer. Talk to a military spouse who lost their partner to the war. These are hardships that cut a person to the core of their existence. Failing is not a hardship. It is a blessing. You have the luxury of living in a country where you can try something and fail and get back up and do it again. You have been given a precious gift that you are choosing to either use wisely or waste foolishly.

Imagine the new inventions, explorations, and breakthroughs that are just waiting to be tapped into. But we'll never know if we stay on the same path we started on. Just remember you're going to start your life and end your life in diapers. What you decide to do in between is completely up to you.

When we're little, we get awards for everything. We have medals that cover every inch of our room, accolades, ribbons, certificates, you name it. We celebrate the small victories. There are pre-school graduations, honor society inductions, perfect attendance awards and much more. We live in the special moments. Then, we become adults. In adulthood, we don't receive accolades. We barely get an "Atta, girl!" every now and then. Things change. We stop celebrating our success. We go about our day without really relishing in what we do well. In order to celebrate your wins, you don't need massive accomplishments. It doesn't have to be giant for it to be meaningful. Own your every day.

Why do we think that everything in our life has to be this massive accomplishment? Why do we let these dangerous thoughts enter our heads that in order to be worthy, it must hold immense weight? All great things come from small accomplishments strung together. Changing your life doesn't mean that you need to change your job, your spouse, your kids, or any other major factor. Everyday courage is made up of small things. Small things that lead to more things that eventually change your life. You're too afraid to change your life because you think it will require too much work. You're afraid to change your life because you think it's not possible. You're afraid to change your life because you are scared of who you may alienate along the way. Changing your life will take less work than you think. Changing your life can happen at any moment. If you alienate people along the way, they aren't meant to be on this journey with you for the long run.

You don't need to be a celebrity or a public figure to make an impact on the world. You don't need millions of dollars and a team of one hundred employees under you to change the world. You are enough. You've always been enough. You can impact the world. I am literally typing this book in Word 2013 on a Dell Inspiration 3520. If you aren't sure what that means, it means this computer is as old as a dinosaur and my Word hasn't been updated since 2013. I have a playroom filled with toys, two toddlers arguing in the background, and a mountain of laundry that needs to be done. I argue with my husband about who's going to walk the mile to get the trash at the end of our street. And I'm most likely serving chicken for dinner for the third consecutive night this week. I spend most nights in the kitchen being my children's snack slave and packing lunches. We don't have maids, nannies, or cleaning ladies. (Although I am totally jealous of you if you do. Way to go.) Sometimes I get really fancy and order Instacart groceries to be delivered to my door while my children sleep. I feel like quite the queen when that glorious human drives up my driveway delivering dinner. It's not glamorous. We don't have the latest tech gadgets or brand-new cars. We pack our lunches for work and try to not spend too much on Christmas. We put money toward student loan debt and cook at home as much as possible. Sometimes the routine of it all can wear me down. Sometimes I want to drive in my car and not stop driving until I see something different. My life isn't bad by any stretch of the imagination, but it isn't fancy.

I am a thirty-something woman trying to find balance in wife-hood, motherhood, and self-hood. I try to have a healthy balance of all three, but most days, they are lopsided. I don't have the secret to life. I don't have the recipe that will help you be the best person ever. I don't have a tips and tricks guide for how to get your kids to listen. I don't have a magical formula that will help you love yourself. All I have are the experiences and lessons that I have learned throughout my life. All of them teaching me something and helping me grow in the process.

Everyday courage isn't the next greatest invention or trip to the moon. Everyday courage isn't finding the cure to cancer or developing a new computer system. Everyday courage is found in homes just like yours. Everyday courage is choosing to be brave when we are scared. Everyday courage is working toward a better version of you. Everyday courage isn't a destination—it's a daily choice. Now go get after it. I'm rooting for you.

ACKNOWLEDGMENTS

In order to achieve great things, one must first believe that better could exist. I wrote the introduction for this book when my son was three months old and finally finished it when he was five. This book is the one that I would have wanted to read when my children were babies.

All great things take time. Don't ever choose to shy away from your dreams because of the time that will take you to achieve them. The time will pass anyway. Strive for greatness. When your time is up and you look back on your life, make sure you have something to be proud of. Possibilities are endless if we have the desire to achieve them.

To God, for putting this desire on my heart to write my own story in the hopes of inspiring other women to do the same.

To my former self, you have come such a long way from the unsure wife, mother, daughter, and friend you once were. Keep growing.

To my husband, for believing I can succeed at anything I put my mind to.

To my firstborn, for giving me the plethora of experiences you will find throughout the pages of this book.

To my strong-willed second child, who has turned my world upside down in the best possible way.

To the mama reading this book, there is no greater love or harder job than that of a mother. I hope this book serves you well.

To all my family, friends, coworkers, authors, and acquaintances along the way, this book could not have been completed without your love and support.

To Page Publishing, for allowing writers a space to publish their work and an audience who is ready to read it.

You have all empowered me to achieve my wildest dreams. And for that, I am forever grateful.

ABOUT THE AUTHOR

Jennifer Hendrix grew up in central Illinois. She graduated summa cum laude from Bradley University with a degree in organizational communication and minors in political science and leadership studies. Jennifer is a risk management consultant by day and a wife and mother by night. Most days she is talking with farmers about the grain market or telling her children to stop fighting while running on the treadmill. Her days are filled with piles of laundry, dirty dishes, dinner preparation, packing lunches, and every now and then, happy hour with her close girlfriends. She loves fresh sheets, warm towels, coffee, wine, and lipstick. She wholeheartedly believes that music was better in the 1990s, and Ja Rule is still her favorite rapper. She doesn't know how to work the television in her home despite continual lessons from her loving husband. She is geographically challenged and uses landmarks instead of compass points. She does her best thinking in the shower, and she always sleeps in socks. She once won a Hula-Hooping competition at the middle school talent show and was a proud member of the Royal Twirling

Academy. She still sings the ABCs when alphabetizing paperwork and has no idea whether cold or hot air is needed when the windows of the car fog up. Wrapping gifts is one of her favorite pastimes. She carries a notebook in her backpack at all times just in case a new idea pops in her head. She is an avid runner, having completed a full marathon, half marathon, and countless 5K's in between. She is a motivational speaker. Jennifer is happily married to her husband of nine years. They live in Southern Illinois with their two children; whom without, this book would not have been made possible.

For more inspiration, please follow the author's Facebook page @realeverydaycourage.

CPSIA information can be obtained
at www.ICGtesting.com
Printed in the USA
LVHW092024040920
664818LV00009B/748

9 781647 018801